Series/Number 06-017

ELECTORAL SUPPORT
FOR IRISH
POLITICAL PARTIES 1927–1973

Michael Gallagher
University of Strathclyde, Glasgow

ERRATA

In Table 1, page 18, and Table 4, page 31, the heading for column 5 should read: R^2

Page 63, line 24 on should read: The method used will be to correlate the parties' support in each of a number of areas of the country for all pairs of elections between June 1927 and 1965. A high correlation between a party's support at two elections indicates that its relative strengths in areas across . . .

Pages 70-71, Note 4 should read: The derivation of the equations was outlined in Section I. The coefficients presented are the semi-standardized coefficients, and relate standard deviation units of the ecological variables to percentage units of the dependent variable. Thus, for example, in June 1927 an increase in the proportion of Irish speakers of one standard deviation of that variable corresponded to an increase of 1.16 percent in Fianna Fail's strength, while an increase in the proportion of farmers of one standard deviation of *that* variable corresponded to an increase of 2.56 percent in Fianna Fail's strength.

For information address

SAGE PUBLICATIONS Ltd.
44 Hatton Garden
London EC1N 8ER

SAGE PUBLICATIONS, INC.
275 South Beverly Drive
Beverly Hills, California 90212

ISSN 0305-3482

International Standard Book Number 0-8039-9860-0

Library of Congress Catalogue Card No. L.C. 76-14523

FIRST PRINTING

Copyright © 1976 by SAGE Publications Ltd.

Printed by Biddles Ltd, Guildford, Surrey

CONTENTS

LIST OF TABLES

Electoral Support for Irish
Political Parties 1927-1973

MICHAEL GALLAGHER

I INTRODUCTION

Politics in the Republic of Ireland have tended to receive scant attention from the academic world, and until six years ago there existed neither a standard work on modern Irish politics nor an adequate history of the state since independence. Although these omissions have since been rectified (see Chubb, 1974 and Lyons, 1971), and despite a recent increase in publications dealing with the country's politics, a large number of lacunae remain. This paper, which seeks to examine the social bases of the support given to political parties in the Irish Republic at general elections since 1927, represents an attempt to fill one of these.

Irish[1] parties are notoriously difficult to classify according to categories into which parties in most other Western democracies can be fitted. The distinguishing feature of Irish politics is the absence of any clear underlying cleavage. Ireland's class-based party (Labour) rarely wins more than 15 percent of the votes; neither of the two main parties — Fianna Fáil and Fine Gael — has a clear class base. There are no religious divisions, whether Catholic/Protestant or clerical/anti-clerical, in the politics of the Republic, for the country is 95 percent Catholic and the great majority of

Author's Note: This paper grew out of research undertaken for an M.Sc. dissertation submitted to the University of Strathclyde in 1974. I wish to thank the following members of the Politics Department there: Tom Mackie, for supervising my work on the dissertation; Professor Richard Rose for advice on effecting the metamorphosis from M.Sc. dissertation to SAGE Paper; and Dr William Miller for advice on statistical techniques. Naturally none of the above should be held responsible for any aspect of my methodology, presentation, interpretations or conclusions. I should like to thank LFC for general encouragement, and acknowledge the financial support of the Social Science Research Council throughout the period in which this research was carried out.

the population are practising Catholics.

Only in North America do comparable party systems seem to exist. The United States, like Ireland, has two parties born (at least in their present forms) in a civil war, but in other respects the two systems differ importantly. The United States has no stable third party, and its regional, economic and ethnic diversity make party loyalties much more complex than in a small, fairly homogeneous country like Ireland. Canada has two large parties which lack obvious class bases, as well as a relatively small but apparently permanent socialist party. In these respects it resembles Ireland, but again important differences exist. Support for both the Liberals and the Conservatives has distinct regional bases, Quebec and Ontario, respectively, being their traditional bastions. In addition, conflict between federal and provincial levels of government and between provinces constitute elements clearly absent from the Irish system.

The Founding of the Irish Party System

The unusual, if not unique, nature of the Irish political party system may be explained by the dramatic events surrounding its foundation. Fianna Fáil and Fine Gael owe their existence to a split in the nationalist movement in the early 1920s. When the Anglo-Irish Treaty was signed in December 1921, Sinn Féin, which had won an overwhelming majority of the seats in the twenty-six counties at the 1918 election, divided over the question of whether or not the Treaty was acceptable. A majority in the Dáil and in the country was prepared to regard it as the best settlement which could be achieved and, as Collins put it, 'freedom to achieve freedom'. To a sizeable minority, however, it was unacceptable, because it seemed to require Dáil members to renege on their 1919 pledge to an Irish Republic.

Sinn Féin's sole raison d'être was the alteration of the constitutional relationship between Ireland and Britain; consequently it embraced members of all classes and most political interests. Social differences remained latent because of the party's preoccupation with the national question. An eventual split in Sinn Féin was almost inevitable; that the split came over the Treaty rather than over some socio-economic question in a post-independence state clearly reduced the possibility of the emergence of 'normal' class-based politics.

In the event, the bitterness of the civil war fought between the armed representatives of the pro- and anti-Treaty groups ensured that the Treaty split would remain unbridgeable for decades to come. The cleavage between the two sides became the basis of the political system, and the parties to which it gave rise have remained, in the view of many commentators, generally devoid of ideological features ever since, even though the Treaty itself has not been a debating point between the parties since the 1930s.

After the Dáil (the Parliament) voted in January 1922 to accept the Treaty, the pro-Treaty forces gained control of the organs of government. After the death of Griffith and Collins's assassination in the summer of 1922, the leadership devolved upon W. T. Cosgrave. In April 1923 a party was formed by those Dáil members who supported his government; it took the name Cumann na nGaedheal (Manning, 1972 : 10).

The anti-Treatyites, led by Eamon de Valera, fought the 1923 election as the Republican Party. They won 44 seats but refused to take them, since they did not recognize the legitimacy of the Free State Parliament set up under the Treaty's provisions. By 1925, however, some of the party's leaders had come to feel that abstentionism should be dropped. A special conference of Sinn Féin in March 1926 rejected a motion proposed by de Valera which would have permitted the party's representatives to enter the Dáil should the Oath of allegiance to King George V be removed, and he led his followers out of the party. Two months later he founded Fianna Fáil (Pyne, 1969: 33-47; Fianna Fáil, 1960 : 10-13).

The Labour Party, the oldest of the three main parties, was only peripherally involved in these events. It can be said to have been formed in 1914, when the Irish Trade Union Congress added 'and Labour Party' to its name (Mitchell, 1974 : 40), but its organization at the local level was generally weak and in many areas it existed only on paper. It did not contest a general election until 1922, when 17 of its 18 candidates were elected. For many years after 1916 the predominance of the national question made it difficult for the party to make its presence felt. It accepted the Treaty, albeit with reservations, and thus, unlike the Republicans, was prepared from the first to grant legitimacy to the state.

The Support for Irish Political Parties: the Literature

There is general consensus among the authorities on the social bases of support for Irish parties, although their evidence has in most cases been only impressionistic. The two main parties owed their origins to the Treaty split, and it is generally agreed that there was a pronounced class component in this division, although one writer has maintained that the split was initially a vertical one, with supporters of each side being 'drawn indiscriminately from all classes of the community', and became horizontal only during the 1930s (Mansergh, 1934 : 286).

Thus Warner Moss (1933 : 19) suggested that the poorer members of society, especially the small farmers in the west, supported the anti-Treaty forces at first, and McCracken's (1958 : 114) view is that de Valera had the allegiance of small farmers, shopkeepers and sections of the 'artisan and labourer classes'. Ayearst (1971 : 47) suggests that radical members of Sinn Féin were opposed to the Treaty because it represented a compromise with the old Ascendancy. Rumpf (1959 : 67-71, 79-86) has demonstrated that the strength of the Republicans at the 1922 and 1923 elections seemed to vary inversely with the degree of 'anglicization' of constituencies, as measured by such factors as the average size of farms, the ratio of farm labourers to farmers, and the proportion of non-Catholics. The most convincing evidence on the point, however, comes from Pyne's (1970 : 243-4) ecological analysis of the Sinn Féin (or Republican) party vote at the 1923 election. He concludes that the party

> was supported by the less well-off sections of the agricultural community, whose housing conditions were far from ideal and who were considerably affected by emigration . . . It appears that the Third Sinn Féin Party had little support from city dwellers, university graduates, non-Catholics and large farmers . . . It was not strongly supported by the industrial proletariat, who were largely confined to the cities, nor by non-agricultural workers throughout the country . . . Sinn Féin in 1923 was largely the party of the rural lower-middle class, the party of the owner-occupiers and small shopkeepers and traders, the party of the people who were, perhaps, the most vulnerable to eoconomic recession.

Professor Chubb (1974 : 77) writes that during the 1920s and 1930s 'the Fianna Fáil program evoked an instictive response from the landless laborers and the land-hungry, from the former poor countryman who had become an urban worker, and from some of the middle class who had hauled themselves up from a rural small-farmer background'. From the early 1930s, he adds, 'Fianna Fáil added to its radical and republican base the support of a growing Catholic commercial and industrial middle class mainly composed of operators of small family businesses'. A publication of the party attributes its victory in the 1933 election to the firm support of the small farmers (Fianna Fáil, 1960 : 21), while Moss (1933 : 136-9) mentions shop assistants, labourers, and the sons and daughters of occupiers as supporters of Fianna Fáil in the early 1930s. Murphy (1969 : 151) believes that many Protestants and ex-Unionsists started to support the party from the 1938 election, while Ayearst (1971 : 222) claims that these voters 'have tended to vote for Fianna Fáil in recent elections'. Sacks (1970 : 536) reports that in 1969 Fianna Fáil was estimated to win the votes of two-thirds of the Protestants in Donegal.

Nowadays, in Chubb's view, both Fianna Fáil and Fine Gael are 'catch-all' parties and thus derive support from all sections of the community, with Fianna Fáil drawing upon a 'great reserve of instinctive loyalty, primarily from small farmers' (1974 : 81). Viney and Edwards (1969 : 96) agree that 'voting support for Fianna Fáil has rested on no class identity' and suggest that the party derives its electoral support from 'the traditional nationalist vote', and, as a result of its long periods in power, from 'the resourceful, entrepreneurial Irishman, especially of the rural and less prosperous areas'.

Turning now to the main opposition party, there is widespread agreement that Cumann na nGaedheal, the forerunner of Fine Gael, was supported by the more prosperous sections of society, who are believed to have generally supported the Treaty (Clarkson, 1926 : 450; Pyne, 1970 : 242). The party is said to have been favoured by the business world, medium and large farmers, the majority of the clergy and the leaders of all the churches, and professional people (Chubb, 1974 : 81-2; Coogan, 1966 : 37; Lyons, 1971 : 519; O'Leary, 1961 : 17). Chubb (1974 : 82) also believes that it was supported faute de mieux by 'members of the former Irish Parliamentary Party and former Unionists', and Mansergh (1934 : 284) too speaks of ex-Unionists' increasing support for the party during the 1920s. Moss (1933 : 137, n.53) describes Cosgrave as 'very proud of his achievement in winning over some of the ex-Unionists to the Irish cause', while it was a common claim of Fianna Fáil that Cumann na nGaedheal was under the control of the ex-Unionists.

The most valuable evidence comes from Moss, who visited Ireland during 1930. Suggesting that the party's support derived from the wealthy in general, the established petit bourgeoisie, small shopkeepers and army pensioners (1933 : 134-37), he gives many illustrations of the conservative nature of Cumann na nGaedheal's appeal. The Chambers of Commerce were said to lean towards the party (p. 58) and its newspaper, *The Star*, was aimed (in the words of its general secretary) at 'the clergy, teachers, professional men and intelligent business people and farmers' incidentally it lost money. The affiliation fee for local Cumann na nGaedheal branches was four times greater than that for the corresponding Fianna Fáil bodies (p. 91), and Moss estimated its annual expenditure as equal to the combined expenditures of Fianna Fáil and Labour (p. 90). In addition, preferring not to contest local elections under its own name, it sometimes fought them as the 'Business Men's Party' (p. 101). Mansergh (1934 : 284, 286) also emphasizes the extremely conservative outlook of Cumann na nGaedheal. Moss (1933 : 54, n.1) describes the party's method of building up new branches in the following terms:

Sometimes Cosgrave's opponents did not realize that his party was actively engaged in campaign work. Cosgrave's party, Cumann na nGaedheal, often carried its organization into new areas by merely sending letters to influential men asking their aid. They went about quietly, often making use of social groups which already existed, and then by election time they had an organization.

Not only was this rather undercover method of recruitment partly responsible for the party's decline during the 1930s and 1940s; it also ensured that it was primarily acquaintances of the local notables, and thus persons from the more prosperous sections of the community, who were recruited into the party.

Chubb believes that, since the Treaty division faded into the past and the major parties became catchall parties, Fine Gael's support has been as broad as Fianna Fáil's but 'thinner on the ground' (1974 : 82). Viney and Edwards (1969 : 96-98), on the other hand, argue that Fine Gael's support comes from 'the commercial and professional middle class' and, increasingly, from 'recent entrants to the lower middle class' and from those who regard the strength of Gaelic culture in rural areas as a handicap to Ireland's attempts to advance economically and technologically. Ayearst (1971 : 62) believes that Fine Gael is 'backed at the polls by electors who have long held to a tradition of voting the Fine Gael label or who support a Fine Gael candidate because of personal rather than party loyalty'.

As most commentators have observed, until the mid-1960s Labour's support came predominantly from rural areas. Manning (1972 : 80) writes that 'it is difficult to see any common patterns' in the constituencies in which it has had 'something approaching consistent representation' and suggests that in many of them 'the Labour T.D. owed his seat as much, if not more, to his personal popularity and record of service as to his allegiance to the Labour Party'. Busteed and Mason (1970 : 374) also believe that most of Labour's T.D.s (i.e. Members of Parliament) 'were returned on the basis of personality and prestige rather than policies', and numerous other examples of such views could be quoted.

At the same time, several writers, while not rejecting this point of view, impute some sort of socio-economic component to the party's support. Chubb (1974 : 83) points out that Labour has been strongest in those areas possessing the largest number of farm labourers, and farm labourers are mentioned as a source of the party's support by several other writers (Inglis, 1965 : 214; McCracken, 1958 : 217; Moss, 1933 : 39; Viney and Edwards, 1969 : 99). Viney and Edwards and McCracken suggest also that small farmers have tended to give some support to the party, and Warner Moss too says (1933 : 74) that small farmers and fishermen formed the principal support of many Labour T.D.s in the early 1930s. Another important pillar of this support, he suggests (1933 : 136), were trade unionists, especially teachers, postmen and railway employees. On the other hand, as Murphy (1969 : 154-55) has pointed out, although Labour may well have suffered from a trade union image which precluded its attracting much left-wing middle-class support, 'it was painfully obvious that the general body of trade unionists did not give their allegiance to the party'.

Survey research into the relationship between social, economic and religious factors and partisanship in the Republic of Ireland is still in its infancy. No surveys asking for respondents' party preferences were carried out before 1969, and only four have been conducted altogether. A Gallup Poll survey of 1969, has been extensively analysed by Whyte (1974 : 630-43).

Fianna Fáil, according to the survey, wins support fairly evenly from all classes, from a minimum of 37 percent from the upper and middle classes to a maximum of 53 percent from small farmers. When the six sub-groups used are collapsed into three larger groups, the evenness of its support becomes even more apparent — it was favoured by 45 percent of the middle classes, 42 percent of the working class and 42 percent of farmers. A clear majority of its supporters in all classes favoured the revival of the Irish language.

The same survey suggests that, in 1969, Fine Gael was strongest amongst the wealthiest sections of Irish society; 46 percent of the large farmers interviewed said they would vote for Fine Gael, as opposed to only 26 percent of small farmers, and among non-farmers it was stronger in the higher social groups than in the lower ones. Overall the survey showed it to have the support of 28 percent of the middle classes, 16 percent of the working class and 40 percent of the farmers.

The survey showed Labour's support to come mainly from the working class — the party drew the support of 14 percent of the middle classes, 28 percent of the working class, and only 3 percent of farmers. In all classes members of trade unions had a significantly higher tendency to vote Labour than non-unionists, as did those living in council houses. It also received greater than average support from voters with a bare minimum of education and from the young.

Methodology

Insofar as we are interested in the social and economic characteristics of individuals who have supported the various parties over the years, we should use individual-level data as a basis for our conclusions. However, in the absence of pre-1969 surveys, the most suitable method of study is ecological analysis. This involves the analysis of data aggregated at the county or constituency level. The data to be matched consist of the results of elections to Dáil Éireann, broken down by constituency, and of census data for each county. The 'political' variables used are the proportions of the valid votes cast in each constituency won by each party at each election. The ecological variables represent social and economic characteristics of each constituency or county.

Of the various approaches which suggest themselves, the one used here is multiple stepwise regression of the political variable upon a number of the ecological variables. This produces a concise predictive equation, and permits assessment of the predictive power of each independent variable after the effects of more powerful predictors have been controlled for.

A problem posed by the Republic of Ireland as far as ecological analysis is concerned is that there is a small number of constituencies, and hence of units of analysis. Census information is normally available only for the twenty-six counties, Dublin City, Dún Laoghaire and Cork City. Some constituencies, like Carlow-Kilkenny, Laoghis-Offaly, Longford-Westmeath and Sligo-Leitrim, are composed of two counties. In addition, as in Britain, election results are not available for any electoral unit smaller than the constituency. Consequently the number of units available for analysis has been either twenty-four or twenty-five, the exact figure varying slightly as constituency boundaries are revised.

Fortunately, Irish counties vary considerably in their social and economic characteristics. Nevertheless, with only twenty-five cases the number of independent variables must be kept to a minimum, and in general no more than two or three predictors are used in any equation. For each party an attempt was made to find a set of two or three independent variables which together have the most predictive power of any set of the same size. By examining the regression equations for the party over the entire period, with these same few variables as the predictors at each election, it would be possible to compare the strength and direction of the relationship of the party's vote with each.

In most cases this attempt was successful — for Fianna Fáil and Independents it is possible to select three ecological variables which at each election form either the strongest or almost the strongest predictive set which could be found. For Labour two variables are sufficient, and most of the minor parties can be dealt with satisfactorily. No simple set of variables with persisting predictive power could be found for Fine

Gael, however, and it was necessary to use ad hoc equations for many elections when considering Fine Gael's support bases.

In addition it was felt desirable to present the equations in a manner which would permit comparison of the effects of the various predictors for one party over a period of time, and for each party at a particular election. No approach to this is entirely free of problems. Using the ordinary b coefficients yields equations which have a clear intuitive meaning — a unit change in the value of the predictor corresponds to a change of so many percent in the party's strength — but the values of the coefficients are dependent upon the means of the predictors, and so predictors with large means will tend to have low b coefficients regardless of the strength of their correlation with the dependent variable. Use of the beta coefficients overcomes this problem, and permits valid comparisons of the effects of each predictor within the same equation. However, because the beta values measure the relationship between the normalized versions of the two variables, they are not completely satisfactory in that they do not give an indication of the real effect of a change in the value of each predictor upon the party's strength in percentage votes as opposed to standard deviation units. Because the standard deviations of each party's votes vary over time, and the standard deviations of the parties' votes at any election also differ, the appearance of the same beta value in two equations will obscure the fact that a change in the value of the predictor corresponds to very different changes in the actual level of the parties' support if the standard deviations of their votes differ markedly. Consequently, in this paper we have used the semi-standardized coefficients; the intuitive meaning to be placed upon them is that a change of one standard deviation in the value of the predictor tends to be associated with a change of so many percent in the level of the party's support.

The chief disadvantage of using ecological analysis as a means of attempting to draw conclusions about the social bases of support for the parties is that, as is well known, the correlation coefficient obtained from analysis at the aggregate level is not necessarily a guide to the corresponding figure at the individual level (see Robinson, 1950).

The 'ecological fallacy', the ascription to individuals of traits manifested at the aggregate level, arises from the difference between the units of observation and the units of inference. Strictly speaking, conclusions can be drawn only about the units of observation. Since in this paper the unit employed is the constituency (and sometimes the county) it follows that no direct conclusions can be drawn about the voting behaviour of individuals. But while this must be borne in mind, it is not necessary to eschew speculation about individuals' behaviour. As Galtung (1967 : 45) has pointed out, 'in general the "fallacy of the wrong level" consists not in making *inferences* from one level of analysis to another, but in making direct *translation of properties or relations* from one level to another, i.e. making too simple inferences'. A correlation at the aggregate level requires explanation, and one way of explaining it is to advance the hypothesis that it is reflected at the individual level. Consequently, while conclusions will be drawn only about which social and economic features of constituencies seem to affect a party's support, explanations of suggested underlying individual-level relationships will sometimes be sought.

It has not always been possible in this paper to retain the constituency as the unit of analysis. In each case the data has been broken down for the smallest unit possible. In other words, where a Dáil constituency comprises two counties, the census data for the two counties have been merged and related to the constituency, while in cases where a county contains more than one constituency the results from each have been added together.

For each election the census data have been related to the votes cast for the three main parties and for Independent candidates. Minor parties have been considered only when they put up candidates in a sizeable number of constituencies and obtained a non-trivial share of the votes cast. In practice the use of this criterion has resulted in six such parties being considered: the National League in June 1927, the Farmers Party in June and September 1927, Sinn Féin in June 1927, 1957 and 1961, the Centre Party in 1933, Clann na Talmhan from 1943 to 1948 and Clann na Poblachta from 1948 to 1954.

For each election the findings of the census closest in time have been used, i.e. for the two 1927 elections the 1926 Census Report, for the elections of 1932, 1933, 1937 and 1938 the 1936 Census Report, for the 1943, 1944 and 1948 elections the 1946 Census Report, for the elections of 1951 and 1954 the 1951 Census Report, for the 1957 and 1961 elections the 1961 Census Report, and for the 1965 election the 1966 Census Report.

The elections for which an ecological analysis of the parties' support has been carried out are the fourteen held between June 1927 and 1965 inclusive.[2] The two most recent elections, those of 1969 and 1973, have had to be excluded from this part of the analysis because the 1969 Electoral Act effected such sweeping changes in constituency boundaries that in many cases these bore little relation to county boundaries. There were only eight areas for which direct comparisons are possible, namely Dublin City, Cork City, Dublin County, Laoghis-Offaly, Limerick,

Longford-Westmeath, Mayo and Wicklow. In addition, the differences between the two sets of boundaries in the cases of Counties Cork and Kerry were negligible. In the remaining cases, however, units of analysis would have had to be created by amalgamating several counties into four much larger units. One would have contained the counties of Tipperary and Waterford, a second Carlow, Kilkenny and Wexford, a third Kildare, Louth, Meath, Cavan and Monaghan, and the fourth Donegal, Leitrim, Sligo, Roscommon, Galway and Clare. This would have produced fourteen units for analysis. Not only would the number of cases have been perhaps intolerably low, but also the merging of counties with such different social, economic and political features as Kildare, Louth, Cavan and Monaghan would have reduced the value of the exercise still further.

An analysis has in fact been carried out by Busteed and Mason (1970), who made an attempt to discover Labour's sources of support at the 1969 election. However, they used only twelve cases in their analysis, from which they excluded thirteen counties and the South Riding of Tipperary. The exclusion of over half the counties of Ireland must call into question the validity of their conclusions.

Consequently in this paper no ecological analysis will be carried out for the elections of 1969 and 1973, although some attempt will be made to discover whether the trends observed up to 1965 have continued.

The social and economic variables with which the election results are correlated were selected mainly on the ground that they seemed a priori more likely to explain the variance in the parties' votes than any other set of variables. The only other consideration affecting the selection was the ease or otherwise of calculating the required statistic from the data presented in the Census Reports.

Ten variables have been included in the analysis for each election:

(i)   the proportion of the gainfully employed population occupied in the agricultural industry;

(ii)   the proportion of the gainfully employed population out of work;

(iii)   the proportion of employers and managers (excluding farmers) in the gainfully employed population;

(iv)   the rateable value of land per acre;

(v)   the proportion of farmers in the gainfully employed population;

(vi)   the proportion of farm labourers in the gainfully employed population;

(vii)   the ratio of farm labourers to farmers;

    (viii)   the average annual rate of emigration;

    (ix)   the proportion of Irish speakers; and

    (x)   the proportion of non-Catholics.

In addition, five variables have been used for only a part of the period. The proportion of farmers in each constituency (or county) who employ no labourers can be calculated from the 1926, 1936 and 1946 Census Reports, and this variable has been used in the analysis of all elections between June 1927 and 1948 inclusive. The proportion of private dwellings which are rented has been taken from the 1946 and 1961 Census Reports and has been used for the elections of 1943 to 1965 inclusive. The proportion of private dwellings which are owner-occupied and the proportion rented from the local authority are both given in the 1961 Census Report and have been used for the elections of 1954 to 1965 inclusive. Finally, the average income per gainfully employed member of the population in 1960 and 1965 has been calculated for each county and used for the elections of 1957, 1961 and 1965.[3]

The small number of units of analysis restricts the number of predictors which can sensibly be included in any equation; another inhibiting factor is the extent of inter-correlation among the predictors. Were all the predictors included in an equation, multi-collinearity would be a severe problem. At every election, three variables – the proportion of farm labourers, the proportion of Irish speakers and the proportion of non-Catholics – vary more or less independently of each other and of the other ecological variables. The other variables tend to be interrelated to a greater or a lesser degree. In counties where a high proportion of the gainfully employed population works in agriculture, there tends to be a high proportion of farmers, a low ratio of farm labourers to farmers, a low average rateable value of land per acre, a low proportion of rented dwellings, and a low average income. In addition, some variables which are intuitively distinct – the unemployed rate, the proportion of employers and managers, and the rate of emigration – are at most, though not all, elections, fairly strongly correlated with each other and with the above set of predictors, so that agricultural constituencies tend to have low unemployment rates, low proportions of employers and managers and high emigration rates.

In consequence, most of the regression equations include only one from this set of highly inter-correlated predictors, although occasionally it appears that more than one has an independent effect upon a party's strength, in which case they may both be included in the equation. At every election the partial correlations between each political variable and those ecological variables not included in the regression equation, after controlling for those ecological variables which are in the equation, have been studied, so that other significant relationships may be identified if they exist.

Not surprisingly, there has been considerable social change in the Republic during the fifty years covered by this study. The percentage of the population living in towns of more than 1,500 people has risen from 32 percent in 1926 to 49 percent in 1966. The percentage of the labour force in industry has risen from 13 percent in 1926 to 26 percent in 1966, and the percentage in agriculture has fallen over the same period from 51 to 31 percent. The population of the country fell from 2,972,000 in 1926 to 2,884,000 in 1966. This was due to emigration on a massive scale, the estimated figure over the period being 963,000. Emigration has fallen off recently, however. Average annual emigration per 1,000 persons was 5.7 between 1961 and 1966, compared with 13.4 between 1951 and 1956 and 14.8 between 1956 and 1961 (Whyte, 1974 : 623).

II FIANNA FÁIL

The three variables included in the regression equations for Fianna Fáil in Table 1 are the proportions of farmers, the proportion of non-Catholics and the proportion of Irish speakers. The first was an obvious variable to include, since Fianna Fáil's support has generally seemed to rest upon the farming community, and the second was also quite strongly correlated with the party's strength in the early elections, although its salience tended to decrease later. The proportion of Irish speakers is also a very useful predictor, and was more strongly correlated with Fianna Fáil's strength than any of the full set of ecological variables at a majority of the elections between June 1927 and 1965. The problem involved in the use of this variable is that it is less rigidly defined than the others; respondents to the census are simply asked whether or not they are Irish speakers. Consequently both those living in the Gaeltacht and speaking only Irish and some of those who have learnt Irish but whose first language is English are subsumed under the designation 'Irish speakers'. However, the element of subjective assessment involved does not necessarily detract from the value of the variable — it may be indeed that among those who do not speak Irish as their first language, self-assessment as an Irish speaker indicates a certain willingness to identify with the movement to revive the Irish language. Another group of people who live in predominantly English-speaking areas but describe themselves as Irish speakers are 'internal emigrants', persons who have moved from the periphery to the centre and have brought some of the periphery's norms

TABLE 1

Support of Fianna Fáil, Related to Ecological Variables, at Elections 1927-65[4]

Election	Irish speakers	Farmers	Non-Catholics	R^2	F	Percentage vote
1927(1)	1.16 (0.72)	2.56 (4.03)*	-1.10 (0.92)	0.35	3.65*	26.2
1927(2)	2.60 (3.42)*	2.60 (3.70)*	-2.52 (4.22)*	0.54	7.91**	35.2
1932	0.18 (0.01)	5.42 (17.76)***	-4.69 (13.87)***	0.67	13.36***	44.5
1933	2.92 (4.21)*	4.39 (10.76)***	-2.92 (5.01)**	0.64	11.77***	49.7
1937	4.26 (7.13)**	1.39 (0.86)	-0.66 (0.17)	0.40	4.43*	45.2
1938	2.84 (5.87)**	3.07 (7.56)**	-2.68 (5.88)**	0.63	11.37***	51.9
1943	3.27 (7.46)**	-1.89 (2.77)	-0.23 (0.04)	0.31	2.99	41.9
1944	4.72 (8.22)***	-1.63 (1.04)	0.93 (0.38)	0.29	2.76	48.9
1948	1.47 (1.34)	0.85 (0.45)	-1.07 (0.84)	0.19	1.68	41.9
1951	2.76 (5.63)**	-2.14 (3.61)	0.52 (0.27)	0.24	2.16	46.3
1954	4.07 (11.03)***	-2.14 (3.24)*	0.16 (0.03)	0.38	4.00*	43.4
1957	2.62 (2.23)	-3.35 (4.10)*	-0.36 (0.06)	0.19	1.59	48.3
1961	3.57 (8.26)***	-1.96 (2.76)	2.25 (4.19)*	0.32	3.32*	43.8
1965	2.41 (5.19)*	-2.02 (3.76)*	-0.19 (0.05)	0.23	2.08	47.7

F values are given underneath the coefficients, with an indication of significance:
* significant at 0.05 level; ** significant at 0.01 level; and *** significant at 0.001 level.

with them. While it would be unwise to infer too much from a speculative interpretation of the variable, some of these possibilities will be considered again later.

1927-1938;

Between 1927 and 1938 Fianna Fáil advanced from being a party with the support of about a quarter of the electorate and an ambiguous attitude towards the legitimacy of the state to the status of a 'natural' governing party; by 1938 it had won four successive elections, winning more than 50 percent of the votes in the most recent, and fully accepted the state's legitimacy.

As Table 1 shows, the social bases of its support did not vary very much over the six elections held during the 1927-38 period, although some changes from election to election can be discerned. The table tends to confirm the general assumptions made about Fianna Fáil's support during this period. The regression' equations and examination of the full correlation matrix[5] confirm that Fianna Fáil was strongest in relatively agricultural constituencies with a low average rateable value of land, a high proportion of farmers (especially farmers employing no labour) and of Irish speakers, and which suffered high emigration rates. It tended to be weakest where a low proportion of the labour force was employed in agriculture, where unemployment and the proportion of employers and managers were highest, and where non-Catholics were relatively numerous.

Fianna Fáil's strength during this phase was negatively related to the unemployment rate; the simple correlation coefficient r between the two variables had an average value of -0.42, and a noticeable relationship remains even then the three variables in the regression equation are controlled for. This finding may be surprising since Fianna Fáil had the image, at this stage, of being a 'radical' party. While it may again be emphasized that the negative relationship at the aggregate level does not necessarily mean that the unemployed had a low tendency to vote for Fianna Fáil, it does nevertheless seem that the party appeared radical only when compared with the very conservative Cumann na nGaedheal. Examination of Fianna Fáil's 1932 election manifesto (reprinted in Moss, 1933 : 206-9) reveals not only an absence of constructive proposals to deal with unemployment but a total failure even to mention the existence of the problem. Of the eight main points in the document, three were concerned with revising the Treaty, one proposed the creation of an industrial sector by protection if necessary, two concerned agriculture, one promised to 'eliminate waste and extravagance in public administration', and the final point concerned the preservation of the Irish language. The platform can scarcely be called radical, and there seems no reason to suppose that the unemployed should have been attracted by it to Fianna Fáil (cf. Gwynn, 1928 : 281-82, and Pyne, 1970 : 236, who concludes that 'the popularly-held view that the urban proletariat favoured the Republican party is incorrect, and that in fact the reverse was true').

Table 1 reveals also that the relationship between the party's strength and the three variables in the regression equation was weaker in June 1927 and 1937 than at the other elections in the period; the R^2 and F values of the equations are lower, and the F values of the variables are weaker. Additionally, most of the simple correlations with those variables not in the equations are relatively weak at these two elections, suggesting that Fianna Fáil's support was more nearly a cross-section of Irish society in June 1927 and 1937 than at the other four elections.

Although Fianna Fáil was considerably stronger in the most agricultural constituencies than elsewhere at each of these six elections, its strength was rather more evenly spread across the coutnry in June 1927 and 1937. The most agricultural constituencies, where the highest proportion of the labour force is in agriculture and where the ratio of farm labourers to farmers is generally lowest, are Cavan, Clare, Galway, Kerry, Leitrim, Mayo, Roscommon and Sligo.[6] The least agricultural areas are Cork City, Dublin (City and County), Tipperary, Waterford, Wexford and Wicklow.

Between the two elections of 1927 Fianna Fáil gained 9 percent of the votes, but it picked up over 13 percent in the most agricultural areas and only 6 percent in the least agricultural ones. It appears that while both Fianna Fáil and Cumann na nGaedheal made large inroads into the votes won in June 1927 by the minor parties, Fianna Fáil tended particularly to capture the votes which Sinn Féin had won in June.[7] A correlation of Fianna Fáil's gains and Sinn Féin's losses between the two elections produces a coefficient of 0.54 (significant at the 0.001 level); Fianna Fáil made a gain of 9.9 percent in each constituency on average, but it gained an average of 12.2 percent in constituencies where Sinn Féin had stood in June. Correlation of Fianna Fáil's gains and Independents' losses also produces a coefficient of 0.54, showing that Fianna Fáil's gains were greatest where Sinn Féin and Independents lost most votes. It is certainly quite reasonable to suppose that many of those who voted for Sinn Féin in June 1927 supported Fianna Fáil in September 1927. Fianna Fáil had originated, after all, from a division in Sinn Féin, and the two parties' ostensible objectives were the same; they differed only in the tactics they were prepared to employ to achieve these objectives.

Fianna Fáil made a further gain of 9 percent of the votes between

September 1927 and 1932 — after the latter election it was able to form a minority government. It is difficult to make inferences about the previous affiliations of these newly-won voters. Correlating Fianna Fáil's gains with other parties' losses produces only one strong relationship, a coefficient of 0.71 with Labour's losses (significant at the 0.001 level). Labour itself, however, lost little more than 1 percent of the votes; the only party which declined substantially was the Farmers Party, whose vote fell by nearly 5 percent. Fianna Fáil's gains correlate very weakly with the Farmers' losses, as they do with Cumann na nGaedheal's losses ($r = 0.1$), and it may be that the party made gains at the expense of most of the other parties.

Between 1933 and 1937 Fianna Fáil lost votes heavily in the most agricultural areas of the country, but its losses were more moderate elsewhere. This uneven pattern resulted from Fianna Fáil's failure to realize certain fears and hopes which had been entertained when it first gained power, and in particular from its attitudes to the existing institutions of the state, to the border with Northern Ireland, and to industry and agriculture.

There had been a belief in many quarters in 1932 that if Fianna Fáil were elected it would do all it could to destroy the Free State's political institutions. In part this belief was the result of statements made by some of its leaders in the days when opposition to the Treaty was all-important for Fianna Fáil. In 1927 de Valera, speaking of the Dáil, said, 'This house itself is faulty' and Lemass described Fianna Fáil as 'a slightly constitutional party'. Even after becoming a minister in 1932 Lemass was to say that 'the title of this Dáil to legislate for this country is faulty'. The fears aroused by the expression of such uncompromising sentiments were naturally played upon by Cumann na nGaedheal. In their 1932 election address (see Moss, 1933 : 201-5) they offered no policies at all, merely invoking the 'tradition of suffering and sacrifice in the cause of Religion' and giving dire warnings of the likely consequences of victory for Fianna Fáil. De Valera's policies, the address contended, would 'result in the destruction of our state institutions' and hence the 'Stability, Religious, Economic, and Financial' of the previous ten years. This would be succeeded by 'sporadic Revolution, Irreligion, Poverty and Chaos — the chief and well-known marks of those countries which experiment in Constitutent Assemblies and changes of regime'. The country would thus be opened to 'those doctrines of Materialism and Communism which can so effectively poison the wells of Religion and National Traditions'. The document also spoke of 'the intense political agitation and unrest which necessarily accompanies the scrapping of the machinery of the state' (cf.

Munger, 1975 : 18).

By 1937 it had become abundantly clear that these claims were exaggerated and almost hysterical. Fianna Fáil had no desire to destroy the institutions of the state, and the most that could be charged against the party was that it had not always been willing to work harmoniously with the Senate.[8]

In addition, the party had not taken any action to remove the border. Although it promised in its 1932 manifesto that it would 'never cease to protest against the iniquity of the partition of our country ruthlessly cut in two against the wishes of the people', it had made no commitment other than that it would 'by every peaceful means strive to bring it to an end'. While in office none of its actions had suggested an irredentist or adventurist attitude towards the question. Moreover, although immediately after winning power in 1932 Fiann Fáil had released IRA men imprisoned by the previous government under the Military Tribunals Act, relationships between the two bodies soon cooled and the IRA was proscribed in June 1936 (Coogan, 1966 : 262-5).

Between 1932 and 1937 the government had also made clear its determination to build up industry in Ireland. Responsibility for this was given to Seán Lemass, the Minister for Industry and Commerce, who was generally regarded as one of its most dynamic ministers. A tariff wall was built and industry began to grow, but at the cost of attracting accusations that the party was neglecting agriculture (Lynch, 1969 ; 75). Moreover, the government's decision to cease handing over to Britain the land annuity payments, and the 'Economic War' thereby precipitated, had led to a sharp fall in exports and a rise in unemployment, with agriculture being hit hardest. The total cost of the 'war' to Ireland was about £48 million.

By 1937 Fianna Fáil had shown that it had no intention of destroying the institutions of the state or of jeopardizing its stability by trying actively to end partition, had concentrated more of its energies on industry than on agriculture, and had exacerbated the depressed state of Irish agriculture by precipitating the Economic War with Britain. It had thus reassured the more industrial regions, while the agricultural areas had suffered most, and it was in these areas that Fianna Fáil lost most ground between 1933 and 1937. It seems that most of the votes the party lost in the most agricultural areas went to Independents, whose share of the votes here rose from under 2 percent to over 10 percent between the two elections. Overall the correlation between Fianna Fáil's losses and Independents' gains is 0.63 (significant at the 0.001 level).

However, Fianna Fáil made up this ground between 1937 and 1938, in the latter election winning almost 52 percent of the votes cast; its gains were due mainly to the termination of the Economic War on terms very favourable to Ireland. Its gains this time were greatest in the most agricultural areas, where it seems that Independents were the losers, for their votes here fell back to below 4 percent. In Clare and Roscommon candidates who had been elected for Fianna Fáil in 1933 stood and were defeated as Independents in 1937 and did not stand in 1938, and in several other constituencies in the most agricultural areas — Kerry South, Leitrim and Sligo — Independents who had polled well in 1937 did not stand in 1938. It may well be that, as in September 1927 and 1933, the cost of fighting two elections within a very short period was beyond the resources of many Independents. Over the whole country Fianna Fáil's gains were again strongly related to Independents' losses ($r = 0.65$, significant at the 0.001 level).

1938-1943

Between 1938 and 1943 there took place a major and fundamental change in the social bases of Fianna Fáil's support. Table 1 reveals that, after controlling for the effects of the proportion of Irish speakers, Fianna Fáil's vote actually decreased as the proportion of farmers increased. The proportion of Irish speakers was indeed the only ecological variable with which the party's strength was at all strongly correlated. In complete contrast to the previous six elections, the simple correlations between its vote and such variables as the proportion of the labour force employed in agriculture, the proportion of farmers and the proportion of farmers employing no labour were negative, albeit only weakly so. Examination of the partial correlations shows that, after controlling for the proportion of Irish speakers, Fianna Fáil was weak in constituencies with a large proportion of the labour force in agriculture and with high emigration rates, and strong where the rateable value of land and the ratio of farm labourers to farmers were high. The proportion of non-Catholics in each area, which at the first six elections was generally quite strong (and negatively) correlated with the party's support, had a negligible effect upon its strength at this and most of the subsequent elections.

Thus, Irish speakers apart, in 1943 Fianna Fáil was not drawing much more support from any one section of the country than from any other. As Table 2 shows, it was very slightly stronger in the least agricultural constituencies than in the most agricultural ones. In terms of its support, the Fianna Fáil of 1943 could certainly be described as a 'catchall' party, at the aggregate level at least.

The party's share of the votes fell in every constituency between 1938

TABLE 2
Breakdown of Fianna Fáil's Strength at 1938 and 1943 Elections

	1938	1943
Most agricultural constituencies	60.01	42.44
Intermediate constituencies	49.47	40.66
Least agricultural constituencies	48.53	42.71
All constituencies	51.93	41.87

and 1943, but the table reveals that these losses were far heavier in the most agricultural areas, where its strength fell by almost 18 percent, than elsewhere. Its enormous losses in these areas were probably caused by a feeling among electors there that Fianna Fáil no longer represented their interests. Chubb (1974 : 81) speaks of 'a growing realization that the party was losing its radicalism and becoming as much a businessman's party as a poor man's party', and Manning (1972 : 99) refers to 'dissatisfaction with the rate of progress under Fianna Fáil and a feeling that the western areas were being neglected'. Certainly, this was a period of depression in the west. Agricultural prices remained static, stocks were depleted by disease, the effects of the Economic War were still being felt, and the British were not prepared to pay as much for Irish agricultural produce as they had been before the war (Meenan, 1969 : 22-23; Murphy, 1969 : 156).

Although some of these problems were obviously outside the government's control, the feeling remained that Fianna Fáil was not doing all it could to alleviate the plight of the small farmers. Betweeen 1938 and 1943 the party became much closer to commerce. O'Leary (1961 : 36) identifies 1938 as the year after which Fianna Fáil's outlook 'took on an increasingly conservative colour'. Murphy (1969 : 150) suggests that

By 1938, while still managing to give the impression of being *the* party for the under-privileged, and so retaining a wide base of support, it was at the same time ... beginning to attract the men of property and position who had originally attached themselves to the pro-Treaty side ... Fianna Fáil's industrial protectionist policy had deeply involved it with the world of business, and the pressure of businessmen in the party helped to modify its initially radical policies.

Its ability to project different but convincing images to different sections of the community seems to have deserted it by 1943.

As we saw earlier, there were signs in 1937 that the loyalty of the most agricultural areas to Fianna Fáil was not unshakeable, but the party regained the lost votes in 1938, largely because there was simply nowhere else for them to go. An outlet did exist, however, in 1943. Clann na Talmhan had been formed in 1938 with the explicit aim of representing the interests of small farmers, and had continued to organize throughout the war years. Although most of the votes Fianna Fáil lost in the most agricultural constituencies almost certainly went to Clann na Talmhan, disaffection with the party in these areas was such that it lost heavily even where no Clann na Talmhan candidate stood; its heaviest loss — 33 percent of the votes was in — Leitrim, where the beneficiaries were Independents. It would appear that discontent with Fianna Fáil was fairly widespread throughout the area, and that Clann na Talmhan gave expression to this mood rather than instigating it.

1943-1965

The profound change which occured between 1938 and 1943 in the bases of Fianna Fáil's support was not reversed during the period 1943-65, as Table 1 indicates. The best predictor of the party's strength was almost invariably the proportion of Irish speakers, and there was generally an inverse relationship with the proportion of farmers. At most of these elections the inclusion of the religious variable contributed very little to the predictive power of the regression equation. The F values of only two of these equations are significant at even the 0.05 level (although those for 1943 and 1944 would have been significant at this level had the religious variable not been included).

Despite fluctuations from election to election, the proportion of Irish speakers was in most cases a significant predictor of the party's strength. Of the three major parties, Fianna Fáil has always been most closely associated with the revival of the Irish language, and is the only party still to support the policy of compulsory Irish in the schools. On these grounds alone, it could be expected that Irish speakers, both those in the Gaeltacht who do not wish to see a further erosion of the position of their language and those who have learnt Irish and regard the restoration of the language as an important step in the revivial of Gaelic culture, would have a tendency, other things being equal, to vote for Fianna Fáil. When the lack of precision in the variable's measurement was discussed earlier it was suggested that migrants from the Gaeltacht living in the eastern counties might well consider themselves to be 'Irish speakers'.

Garvin (1974) has argued that Fianna Fáil's dominance of Irish politics is due partly to an 'invasion' of the centre by the periphery, and that Fianna Fáil has successfully brought a rural political style, in which the party machine acts as a broker between citizens and the bureaucracy, into Dublin. Of a sample surveyed, he reports (1974 : 321) that over half of Fianna Fáil activists in Dublin were rural-born, as opposed to only about a third of Fine Gael and Labour activists and the whole Dublin population. It does not necessarily follow that Fianna Fáil in Dublin is therefore especially attractive to migrants from the countryside, but the picture he presents, taken in conjunction with our finding that the party's strength is positively related to the proportion of 'Irish speakers', at least suggests such a possibility.

The negative relationship between Fianna Fáil's support and the proportion of farmers, controlling for Irish speakers, persisted and indeed grew stronger during ther period. Although at the 1943 and 1944 elections the relationship was only weak, and in 1948 was slightly positive, at four of the next five elections the variable was significant at the 0.05 level. Fianna Fáil, then, did not during this period regain the dominant position it had earler enjoyed among the farming community.

There was no reversion to the pattern of the earlier period, when Fianna Fáil was much stronger in the most agricultural regions of the country than elsewhere. Between 1943 and 1944 its share of the votes rose by over 7 percent, but its gains were only about 2 percent greater in the most agricultural constituencies than in the least. Moreover, Clann na Talmhan and Independent candidates maintained their strength in rural areas, despite the burden of fighting two elections within such a short space of time and despite Fianna Fáil's appeal for support because of its success in keeping Ireland out of the war. Fianna Fáil's gains seem to have been made mainly at the expense of Fine Gael and Labour, then suffering from internal divisions.

Between 1944 and 1948 Fianna Fáil suffered a loss of 7 percent in its vote, the intervention in 1948 of Clann na Poblachta being the main cause of this. At the next three elections the tendency was for its strength in the most agricultural areas to remain fairly constant, while in the least agricultural areas its support was more changeable. Its gains here followed its periods in opposition, and its losses its periods in government. It seems that voters in the wealthiest and most industrial areas had a greater propensity to desert the outgoing government at elections during the 1950s than did voters elsewhere. The 1950s were a period of austerity for Ireland; prices rose steeply, and at each election the outgoing government was charged with a failure to control inflation. Agriculture, on the other hand, recovered from its earlier depression, and farmers, as producers of food, were less disturbed by inflation than were the consumers.

At the next two elections, however, the changes in Fianna Fáil's strength were very similar all across the country; between 1957 and 1961 it lost no more ground in the least agricultural regions than elsewhere. Partly, no doubt, this was a consequence of the improvement in Ireland's economic fortunes which can be traced to the late 1950s, and became associated with Dr Ken Whitaker. Another cause may well have been the change of leadership in 1959 from de Valera, whose dream, in the words of Rumpf (1959 : 126-27), was of 'a frugal, gaelic Ireland . . . in which there would be neither rich nor poor, but many small farmers and small industries spread over the land', to Seán Lemass. It had been the responsibility of Lemass, as Minister of Industry and Commerce for all but two of Fianna Fáil's many years in power, to realize de Valera's often vague ideas. A T.D. for a Dublin constituency — de Valera sat for County Clare — he understood the viewpoint of industry perhaps better than that of small farmers, and had the image of a 'middle-class mercantilist with little personal feeling for agriculture' (Viney and Edwards, 1969 : 46; cf. Coogan, 1966 : 108-9). In 1965 the party's strengths in the most agricultural, least agricultural and intermediate areas were practically indentical. Between the two elections many of Fianna Fáil's 'old guard' had left the cabinet and had been replaced by young men with the image of technocrats. Paddy Smith, the Minister for Agriculture, resigned in 1964 alleging that Lemass was sacrificing rural to urban interests, and was succeeded by Charlie Haughey, a Dublin T.D. once described as 'the epitome of the men in the mohair suits' (Coogan, 1966 : 109-10). The party's image became still less agrarian. ·

An interesting feature of Fianna Fáil's support at the 1961 election is that the proportion of non-Catholics was a fairly strong and positive predictor. It will be shown in section V that there is evidence to suggest that a number of Protestant votes which before 1961 had gone to Independent candidates were absorbed by the two major parties in 1961.

1965-1973

As was pointed out in section I, ecological analysis of party support is not possible for elections since 1965 because of the constituency boundary revisions of 1969. It is thus necessary to rely upon breakdowns of the parties' votes in various types of constituency.

Table 3 suggests that a change in Fianna Fáil's support has occured since 1965, to give a picture similar to that obtaining at the elections of 1927-38. In both 1969 and 1973 the party was strongest in the most

TABLE 3

Breakdown of Fianna Fáil's Strength at Elections 1965-73

	1965	1969	1973
Most agricultural constituencies	47.86	52.15	52.63
Intermediate constituencies	47.52	45.16	46.37
Least agricultural constituencies	47.70	42.87	43.13
All constituencies	47.67	45.66	46.24

agricultural constituencies and weakest in the least agricultural ones. Although consideration only of the national figures for the last three elections might suggest that the political system is becoming stabilized, with Fianna Fáil 'settling down' at around the 46 percent level, closer examination shows considerable fluctuation at the regional level. Between 1965 and 1969 the party's strength rose by over 4 percent in the most agricultural constituencies, but fell by 2 percent in the country as a whole.

Why did Fianna Fáil make gains in the heavily agricultural regions in 1969 and losses elsewhere? One reason for its losses is that after the heady days of the mid-1960s when the forecasts of the First Economic Programme had proved under-optimistic, those of the Second Programme, as a result of unforeseen circumstances, exceeded the performance of the economy. On the other hand the party had taken steps to restore its appeal to farmers — in 1966 Haughey was promoted from Agriculture to Finance and was succeeded by Neil Blaney, a T.D. of twenty years' standing and with very close connections with the grass roots in his native Donegal.

Not the least important factor was the change in the party's leadership in 1966; Seán Lemass stepped down and Jack Lynch 'emerged' as his successor. It is generally accepted that Irish elections tend to revolve to a large extent around the party leaders' personalities. As Farrell (1971a : 3-4) has put it,

> The leader is the main standard-bearer of the party's fortunes . . . General elections have acquired some of the characteristics of a plebiscite, a political popularity contest, in which the images are personalized through the leaders.

Campaign slogans tend to reflect this, voters being urged to 'Let Lemass Lead On' or to 'Back Jack'. At the time of the 1969 election the mood of the electorate seemed to be flowing against Fianna Fáil, and the party's victory owed much to Lynch's personal appeal. According to Farrell (1971a : 4 and 77-78) 'both commentators and partisans accept . . . that in the 1969 election it was Mr Lynch's own efforts that countered an anti-government trend', and Manning (1972 : 56) writes that 'the strength of Fianna Fáil's organization . . . combined with the inability of the opposition parties to come together and an extremely successful personal campaign by Lynch . . . seemed to turn the tide to Fianna Fáil'.

Table 3 suggests that different currents may have been flowing in different regions. Lynch, although by profession a barrister and a T.D. for Cork City, was less closely associated in the public eye with industry than Lemass had been, and possessed in addition the advantages of having been not only Minister for the Gaeltacht for two years but also one of the most successful Gaelic games players of all time. This last attribute, in particular, may by itself have won votes for Fianna Fáil in rural areas, given the increasing importance of participation in sport, and especially Gaelic sports, as a route of entry into the Dáil (Farrell, 1971b : 320-22).

Between 1969 and 1973 there was little further change in the party's strength, either nationally or regionally; it was almost 10 percent stronger in the most agricultural constituencies than in the least agricultural ones. This is perhaps not surprising, since there were few changes in the composition or the style of the government after 1969. The party's image was seriously affected only by the dismissal of two senior ministers, Haughey and Blaney, and the resignation of two others in May 1970 in connection with a trial concerning the smuggling of arms to the IRA in the north. Although some thought at the time that this, and the government's general support for Britain's handling of the northern troubles, might cause the break-up of the party or at least lose it some of its more republican supporters, there is no evidence that this action cost it any popularity; when a by-election was held in the border constituency of Donegal-Leitrim in December 1970, Fianna Fáil won a higher proportion of the votes than it had at the 1969 election.

III CUMANN NA NGAEDHEAL AND FINE GAEL

For Fine Gael and its forerunner Cumann na nGaedheal there is no set of two or three variables which could be used to assess its bases of support at every election throughout the period. Particular variables appear to be useful predictors of the party's strength at some elections, but are practically valueless at others, while at a number of elections Fine Gael's vote is only weakly related to any of the ecological variables. Rather than retain a fixed set of variables for all fourteen elections, and present insignificant equations for elections when the party's support was in fact more strongly related to other variables, we have generally chosen for each election the set of variables producing the most powerful predictive equations, while attempting to preserve some continuity in the selection to enable long-term trends to be identified.

1927-1933

Fine Gael was not formed until after the 1933 general election, and in this section we shall consider the bases of support for Cumann na nGaedheal at the elections of 1927, 1932 and 1933. Cumann na nGaedheal, sometimes known as 'the Cosgrave Party', was in power between 1922 and 1932. It never won a majority of seats in the Dáil or indeed came within a dozen seats of doing so, always relying upon the support of minor parties, especially the Farmers Party and Independents, but retained office because it was the largest single party in the Dáil up to 1932. In August 1927 the government survived a vote of no confidence only on the casting of the Speaker.

At the two elections of 1927, the strongest relationship between the party's strength and any of the ecological variables was a negative one with the proportion of farm labourers (see Table 4). At both elections the party tended to win more votes in constituencies with a low proportion of non-Catholics, and there was a fairly strong and negative relationship with the unemployment rate in June and with the emigration rate in September. The relationship with the proportion of employers and managers was weakly negative in June 1927 and only weakly positive in September 1927, but was much stronger, and positive, in 1932 and 1933; at these two elections the negative relationships with the proportions of farm labourers and of non-Catholics persisted.

To some extent, then, this analysis bears out the views presented in the literature on Cumann na nGaedheal's support. The strong positive relationship with the proportion of employers and managers observed at the 1932 and 1933 elections implies that the party won the support of the business world and of the wealthiest sections of society generally. The assertion that it was supported by medium and large farmers is more difficult to test. At all four elections the party was weak in constituencies with a high proportion of farm labourers. In 1932 and 1933 there was a negative relationship between the party's strength and the proportion of

TABLE 4

Support of Cumann na nGaedheal and Fine Gael, Related to Ecological Variables, at Elections 1927-65

Election	Predictor	Predictor	Predictor	R^z	F	Percentage vote
1927(1)	Farm labourers -4.54 (12.15)	Non-Catholics -1.49 (1.27)	Unemployment rate -2.04 (2.44)	0.44	5.29**	27.4
1927(2)	Farm labourers -4.83 (6.50)**	Non-Catholics -2.16 (1.15)	Emigration rate -3.08 (2.30)	0.34	3.45*	38.3
1932	Employers & managers 3.15 (7.05)*‡	Non-Catholics -2.90 (6.11)**		0.33	5.09**	35.3
1933	Employers & managers 3.74 (6.57)**	Non-Catholics -1.97 (1.85)	Farm labourers -2.69 (3.68)*	0.36	3.77*	30.5
1937	Irish speakers -2.04 (1.69)	Non-Catholics -3.47 (4.93)**	Unemployment rate -2.26 (2.30)	0.25	2.18	34.8
1938	Irish speakers -4.67 (8.37)***	Non-Catholics -3.99 (6.42)**	Unemployment rate -3.40 (4.97)**	0.40	4.42*	33.3
1943	Employers & managers 3.19 (5.22)*			0.19	5.22*	23.1
1944	Employers & managers 2.08 (1.48)			0.04	1.48	20.5
1948	Employers & managers 4.73 (11.76)**			0.34	11.76**	19.8
1951	Employers & managers 2.43 (2.52)			0.10	2.52	25.8
1954	Farmers -4.64 (7.95)**			0.27	7.95**	32.0
1957	Employers & managers 1.84 (1.77)			0.07	1.77	26.6
1961	Employers & managers 1.85 (1.89)			0.08	1.89	32.0
1965	Farmers 4.41 (12.57)***	Farm labourers -2.77 (5.09)*		0.46	9.37**	34.1

farmers in each area (r = -0.4) and a positive relationship with the ratio of farm labourers to farmers, a rough indicator of farm size (r = 0.4). In 1932 and 1933, then, it seems that its strength in rural areas was greatest where farm size was large, and the negative relationship with the proportion of farm labourers would at least suggest that this strength derived from farmers wealthy enough to employ agricultural labourers rather than from the labourers themselves.

In other respects the opinions expressed in the literature must be queried. The view that the party was supported by former Unionists is not substantiated by this analysis. Most ex-Unionists were Protestants and Cumann na nGaedheal's strength was inversely related to the proportion of Protestants. Protestants had little reason to support Cumann na nGaedheal despite the 'pro-Empire' image its opponents tried to attach to it, even though it was much less frightening in their eyes than Fianna Fáil. The Catholic Church had whole-heartedly supported the government during the Civil War, and 'the pious William' Cosgrave was if anything a more devout Catholic than de Valera. The party scored a notable seccess after the June 1927 election when it won over the ex-Unionist Major Bryan Cooper to its ranks in County Dublin — part of the process unkindly referred to by Fianna Fáil speakers as 'the alliance of a dog with its fleas' — but even here Gwynn (1928 : 145) suggests that many of those ex-Unionists who had supported Cooper switched their votes at the September 1927 election to a fresh Independent candidate.

In addition, many of the relationships which were strong in 1932 and 1933 were weak at the two elections of 1927, suggesting that the party's support bases may have hardened between 1927 and 1932. In June 1927, indeed, some of the simple correlations were at variance with the later relationships; there were positive relationships with the proportion of farmers (r = 0.23) and of Irish speakers (r = 0.33), and negative relationships with the proportion of employers and managers (r = -0.21) and the ratio of farm labourers to farmers (r = -0.28). At the September election most of the correlations were very weak. Pyne (1970 : 253-57) has shown that Cumann na nGaedheal's strength at the 1923 election was only weakly related to most of the ecological variables he employed in his study, and it may be that Cosgrave's hope, expressed in 1923, that the party would attract pro-Treatyites ('the best elements of the country') 'irrespective of class or creed' was realized to a greater extent than is sometimes supposed, and that only during the late 1920s and the early 1930s did it acquire a more class-based pattern of support.

It must be borne in mind that although Cumann na nGaedheal remained in office up to 1932, its overall strength varied considerably during its existence. In June 1927 it won only 27 percent of the votes. It gained 11 percent at the September 1927 election but by 1933 it had fallen back to 30 percent. Given these fluctuations, it is not surprising that the nature of its support did not remain stable.

A breakdown of the party's support by the strength of agriculture in constitutencies confirms this. In June 1927 the party was stronger by 6.4 percent in the most agricultural constituencies than in the least, but at the next three elections this position was overturned. Between the two elections of 1927, Cumann na nGaedheal advanced by only 6 perccent in the most agricultural areas, but by about 13 percent elesewhere. Gwyn (1928 : 144) asserts that at the September 1927 election many former supporters of the Farmers Party 'rallied to the Government in which they believed' when they appreciated the danger to it constituted by Fianna Fáil's entry into the Dáil, and the figures tend to bear this out, the correlation between Cumann na nGaedheal's gains and the Farmers' losses being 0.44 (significant at the 0.01 level). There was a similar relationship with Independents' losses, but only a weak relationship with the losses of the National League and none at all with those of Sinn Féin. By 1933, Cumann na nGaedheal took 7.2 percent more of the vote in the least agricultural seats than in the most rural.

When the minor party vote slumped between the two elections of 1927, Fianna Fáil was the main beneficiary in the poorest areas and Cumann na nGaedheal picked up the votes in the wealthier areas. The political party system, highly fractionalized in June 1927, began to polarize around the two large parties, with Fianna Fáil's entry into the Dáil pushing the Treaty even more into the forefront of politics and making it more difficult for parties emphasizing economic interests to win votes.

Although Cumann na nGaedheal was forced to leave office after the 1932 election, it is important to remember that this was not so much because former supporters deserted it as because Fianna Fáil made large gains; excluding the Universities, Cumann na nGaedheal lost only 3 percent of the votes and four seats between September 1927 and 1932. Between 1932 and 1933, however, its share of the votes fell by a further 5 percent, and it found itself a long way adrift of Fianna Fáil, by about 20 percent in terms of votes and by twenty-eight seats. The only parties to gain votes between these two elections were Fianna Fáil and the newly-formed Centre Party. Cumann na nGaedheal's losses and Fianna Fáil's gains are not statistically related ($r = -0.05$), but correlations of its losses and the Centre Party's gains produces a coefficient of 0.34 (significant at the 0.05 level). In addition, while the mean two-party swing from Cumann na nGaedheal to Fianna Fáil was 5.2 percent, in constituencies where the Centre Party stood in 1933 the mean two-party swing to it from

Cumann na nGaedheal was 10.1 per cent. The conclusion to be drawn is that although in the most general terms the period from 1927 to 1933 was one of Cumann na nGaedheal decline and Fianna Fáil advance, there was probably very little direct movement of voters between these parties; the switching occurred almost by proxy, through minor parties and Independents.

1933-1948

The period from 1933 to 1948 was one of unrelieved gloom for the party. In September 1933 Cumann na nGaedheal merged with the Centre Party and the National Guard to form Fine Gael, whose president was the National Guard leader General O'Duffy (Manning, 1970 : 92-98). He soon showed himself to be a warm admirer of Fascism as then practised in Italy, and several leading party members expressed the hope that the Corporate State would be introduced in Ireland. O'Duffy's touches of megalomania and apparent willingness to sanction extra-parliamentary tactics brought about his removal from the leadership in September 1934 — he was succeeded by the former Cumann na nGaedheal leader W. T. Cosgrave. This year-long flirtation with Fascism seems to have had little effect on Fine Gael's subsequent outlook, with the possible exception of the almost obsessional hostility of the Blueshirts (the National Guard) to Communism. Indeed, the party put the episode behind it so quickly that, in the words of O'Sullivan (1940 : 474), 'New Fine Gael was but old Cumann na nGaedheal writ small'.

From the mid-1930s until 1948 the party simply declined — it was unable to attract new members, and as Fianna Fáil became more conservative it lost its distinct image. If it had ever won any support from pro-British elements it probably lost much of it after 1942, when its deputy leader resigned after the party had reacted unfavourably to his suggestion that Ireland join the war on the Allies' side. Its share of the vote fell at every election from 35 percent in 1937 to below 20 percent in 1948. It became short of funds and contested only six of the ten by-elections held between 1944 and 1948, without winning any of them — it had great difficulty in finding willing candidates (Whyte, 1971 : 112-13). When Cosgrave resigned the leadership in January 1944 it had an opportunity to try to develop a fresh image, but instead chose as his successor Richard Mulcahy, a *bête noire* to many because of his role as Minister of Defence in the execution of anti-Treatyites during the Civil War and his close involvement with the Blueshirts during the 1930s. Not only observers but even some leaders of the party seem to have felt that Fine Gael was nearing the end of its life (Murphy, 1969 : 153; O'Leary,

1961 : 40). It appeared to have nothing distinctive to offer — most interests could be catered for by other parties. The business world had grown to accept Fianna Fáil, which still had the support of many farmers, while the working classes had the Labour Party to represent them, even if it did not command their whole-hearted support. Those farmers disillusioned by Fianna Fáil's behaviour in office could articulate their demands through Clann na Talmhan. By 1948, then, Fine Gael was firmly rooted in the past, lacklustre, moribund and, as far as policies were concerned, little more than a pale shadow of Fianna Fáil.

Table 4 shows that at both the 1937 and 1938 elections the party's strength was inversely related to the proportion of Irish speakers, the rate of unemployment and the proportion of non-Catholics in each area. The last relationship would cast further doubt upon the view that Fine Gael had the support of former Unionists, but the other two confirm the impession of the party as one with little attraction to the under-privileged or to Irish speakers.

The decisive change in its fortunes occurred between the elections of 1938 and 1943; its overall strength fell from 33 to 23 percent and it lost its image as a 'majority-bent' party. Between 1943 and 1944 its strength fell by a further 3 percent, and it dropped another 1 percent between 1944 and 1948.

Table 4 shows that the party tended to win most votes at each election in constituencies with a high proportion of employers and managers. Many of the relationships observed for its support at the 1937 and 1938 elections still held — its strength was positively related to the rateable value of land and to the ratio of farm labourers to farmers, and negatively related to the proportion of the labour force employed in agriculture, the proportion of farmers, the emigration rate and the proportion of Irish speakers. These relationships were weak in 1944, but had recovered their strength by 1948.

The very heavy losses sustained by the party between 1938 and 1943 were greatest in the most agricultural areas of the country, where it lost over 13 percent of the votes. Its votes went in the main to Clann na Talmhan; correlation of its losses with Clann na Talmhan's gains produces a coefficient of 0.57 (significant at the 0.001 level), and its average loss was 12.4 percent in the constituencies where Clann na Talmhan stood in 1943 as opposed to only 5.7 percent in the others.

Between 1943 and 1948 it declined steadily, if gradually, left with a hard core of supporters who were unlikely to desert it but lacking the ability to attract new support. The appearance in 1946 of Clann na Poblachta does not seem to have accelerated its decline — it is indeed unlikely that this apparently radical and republican party appealed to die-hard Fine Gael supporters. In 1948, then, Fine Gael was dispirited and weak throughout the country, especially in the most agricultural areas.

1948-1965

The years after 1948 saw the 'near-miracle of Fine Gael rehabilitation' (Murphy, 1969 : 162). Fianna Fáil lost eight seats and its majority at the 1948 election, and the Fine Gael leader, General Mulcahy, took the initiative in arranging discussions between the other parties which led to the formation of the first Inter-Party government. Every Dáil grouping apart from Fianna Fáil was given at least one Ministry, but Fine Gael was allocated the largest number and a leading party member, John Costello, became Taoiseach.

The government proved unexpectedly durable and successful, and lasted for over three years. Its collapse was precipitated by divisions in Clann na Poblachta over the 'Mother and Child' affair, although the coup de grâce was administered when two farming deputies withdrew their support. Fine Gael's image was not tarnished by either incident, and it emerged from the experience of government in a much stronger position. At the 1951 election it increased its share of the votes by 6 percent and won nine new seats.

Revived by its period of office, it 'regained its self-confidence (and) turned to the business of organizing itself properly and of interesting youth in the party' (Murphy, 1969 : 163). The revival continued, and at the 1954 election Fine Gael won ten more seats and increased its share of the votes by a further 6 percent. The second Inter-Party government, in which Fine Gael was the major force, held power between 1954 and 1957, but it was less successful than the first and in 1957 the party reverted to its 1951 level of strength.

Mulcahy resigned the leadership in 1959 and was succeeded by James Dillon. After a change in Labour's leadership in 1960, talk of further Inter-Party governments faded, and Fine Gael fought the 1961 and 1965 elections with the expressed aim of forming a government on its own. It made gains at each election, in 1965 winning 34 percent of the votes and 47 seats.

The party's support bases at the elections of 1951, 1954, 1957 and 1961 were essentially similar. At each it drew most support in constituencies with a high proportion of employers and managers and where the rateable value of land was high, and least where the proportion of labour force in agriculture and the rate of emigration were high. This tendency was very marked at the 1954 election, but the relationships were weak at the 1951, 1957 and 1961 elections, as Table 4 shows — at these elections all of the coefficients of correlation between the party's strength and ecological variables had low values, and none of the regression equations is statistically significant.

One relationship which did change importantly over these four elections was that with the proportion of non-Catholics. Having been either negative or very weakly positive at every election up to and including that of 1957, the relationship was positive and the strongest found for Fine Gael's support in 1961 ($r = 0.29$). As will be shown in section V, a change in non-Catholics' voting habits appears to have occurred between 1957 and 1961.

At the 1965 election, however, the basic position was completely reversed; Table 4 illustrates the contrast between the patterns of its support in 1954 and 1965. In 1965 Fine Gael was strongest in constituencies with a high proportion of farmers ($r = 0.58$) and in those with high emigration rates ($r = 0.54$), and weakest where there was a high proportion of employers and managers ($r = 0.23$), where the ratio of farm labourers to farmers was high ($r = -0.50$) and where the average income per gainfully employed member of the population was high ($r = 0.51$). Most of these relationships were equal in strength but opposite in direction to those obtaining in 1954, and it will be shown in section VI that the spatial distribution of the party's strength in 1965 was quite unrelated to its distribution in 1954.

While Fine Gael's share of the votes increases from 19.8 percent in 1948 to 34.1 percent in 1965, its vote did not grow evenly around the country; its greatest gains were in the most agricultural constituencies (+8.7 percent) in 1951 and in the least agricultural areas (+7.5 percent) in 1954. It seems that between 1948 and 1951, when the minor parties' and Independents' share of the votes fell by 11 percent, Fianna Fáil tended to pick up these votes in the wealthier areas while Fine Gael did so in the heavily agricultural regions. Here neither Fianna Fáil's nor Labour's share of the votes altered by more than 1 percent between 1948 and 1951, but Fine Gael's share increased by nearly 9 percent while Independents and minor parties lost 8.4 percent. It would appear that voters here deserting Clann na Talmhan and Clann na Poblachta turned to Fine Gael, the coalition partner of these parties, rather than to Fianna Fáil.

At the three elections in the 1950s, voters in the least agricultural constituencies had a tendency to move away from the outgoing government and switch to the leading opposition party. In 1951 Fianna Fáil made large gains here while Fine Gael's gains were relatively small; in 1954 Fianna Fáil lost most heavily and Fine Gael made its greatest gains were in the most agricultural constituencies (+8.7 percent in 1951 and in the least agricultural areas (+7.5 percent) in 1954. It seem that between 1948 and 1951, when the minor parties' and Independents share of the votes fell by 11 percent, Fianna Fail tended to pick up these votes in the wealthier areas while Fine Gael did so in the heavily agricultural regions. Here neither Fianna Fáil's nor Labour's share of the votes altered by more than 1 percent between 1948 and 1951, but Fine Gael's share increased by nearly 9 percent while Independents and mino parties lost 8.4 percent. It would appear that voters here deserting Clann na Talmhan and Clann na Poblachta turned to Fine Gael, the coalition partner of these parties, rather than to Fianna Fáil.

At the three elections in the 1950s, voters in the least agricultura constituencies had a tendency to move away from the outgoing government and switch to the leading opposition party. In 1951 Fianna Fáil made large gains here while Fine Gael's gains were relatively small in 1954 Fianna Fáil lost most heavily and Fine Gael made it greatest gains here, and in 1957 it was Fine Gael which lost and Fianna Fáil which gained. In this economically difficult period the problem faced by the second Inter-Party government were particularly severe and its response to a rapidly worsening balance of payments problem in 1956 was to increase taxation and cut public expenditure, measures which naturally made it unpopular. Elections during the 1950s were concerned mainly with the question of who was to be given the chance to try to keep down prices and taxes (O'Leary, 1961 : 44-46; Chubb, 1959 : 191-95) and it appears that voters in the wealthier areas had a tendency to vote against the outgoing government in the hope that the opposition would be better able to check the rise in prices.

Between 1961 and 1965 a remarkable change in Fine Gael's suppor occurred. Its share of the votes in the wealthiest constituencies fell slightly and its strength in the intermediate ones hardly changed, but it made gain of more than 10 percent in the most agricultural regions. Between 1957 and 1965, as Table 5 shows, the party gained 14 percent of the vote

TABLE 5

Breakdown of Fine Gael's Strength at Elections 1957-61

Election	Most agricultural constituencies	Intermediate constituencies	Least agrigultural constituencies	All constituencies
1957	24.59	28.86	25.76	26.63
1961	28.69	35.42	30.80	32.02
1965	38.79	35.88	29.50	34.08

here, as opposed to only 7 percent in the intermediate areas and 4 percent in the wealthiest areas.

Why did Fine Gael make such a dramatic advance in the most agricultural parts of the country? Between 1957 and 1965 the votes of minor parties and Independents combined fell by over 20 percent, and it appears that most of these votes were absorbed by Fine Gael. This was, no doubt, partly because of the change in Fianna Fáil's image then taking place as a result of Lemass's accession to the leadership and the party's increasing involvement with industry, but the importance of changes then occurring within Fine Gael itself should not be underestimated. The leadership of the party passed in 1959 from Mulcahy and Costello — Mulcahy was a Civil War veteran who sat for Tipperary, Costello a lawyer sitting for Dublin South-East — to James Dillon, a farmer representing Monaghan. Dillon had been the Minister of Agriculture in the two Inter-Party governments; he had proved to be dynamic and successful, and one of his initiatives, the Land Rehabilitation Project, 'brought the first faint stirrings of hope to many districts long assumed to be stagnant if not dying' (Lyons, 1971 : 546). It was in just these districts that Fine Gael made its largest gains in 1965.

In addition, the party fought the 1965 election on a platform very different from those which had characterized it in the past. Its programme, entitled 'The Just Society', attempted to give Fine Gael the image of a social democratic party, and its social policy, in the words of Viney and Edwards (1969 : 97) 'might more predictably have come from a party of the Left'. It called for more state planning to promote social justice, and attacked Fianna Fáil's emphasis on productive capital expenditure, urging that social expenditure — on housing, for example — be increased. Perhaps conscious of its image as a large farmers' party, it made a direct appeal to the poorest farmers, promising, 'We propose to exempt completely from rates all farmers whose lands and agricultural buildings have a total value of £25 or less' (Fine Gael, 1965 : 13).

Most observers have minimized the electoral impact of this major policy shift by Fine Gael at the 1965 election. Viney and Edwards (1969 : 97) write that 'the incongruity of this programme with the traditional social base of the party may have bewildered the floating voter; Fine Gael gained no new seats', while Manning (1972 : 29) merely comments that it 'had little electoral consequence'. The small change in Fine Gael's overall strength has, however, obscured the very pronounced change in its strength in the poorest regions of the country, as a result of which it was fully 9 percent stronger there than in the least agricultural constituencies.[9]

Fine Gael's gains in the most agricultural areas appear to have been made at the expense of minor parties and Independents. In 1961 both

Clann na Talmhan and Sin Féin won about 6 percent of the votes here — neither stood in 1965, and Independents' votes fell by about 5 percent. Fianna Fáil and Labour each made a gain of about 4 percent here. Minor parties and Independents had won more than 20 percent of the votes in the poorest constituencies at every election between 1943 and 1961, but in 1965 their share fell to 5 percent. For some constituencies it can only be assumed that these groups' decline and Fine Gael's advance between 1961 and 1965 were due to voters switching to Fine Gael, but in others there is little doubt that this is what happened: in Galway East one of Clann na Talmhan's two T.D.s died in 1964, and his son stood and was elected for Fine Gael in the by-election and the 1965 general election, while in Mayo North a candidate moved across from Clann na Talmhan to Fine Gael.

1965-1973

Fine Gael's strength in terms of votes remained steady at around the 35 percent level at the 1969 and 1973 elections, although it gained three seats in 1969 and four more in 1973. The 1973 election was the most successful in Fine Gael's history — it won its highest-ever number of votes, share of votes and number of seats. James Dillon resigned the party leadership immediately after the 1965 election, and was succeeded by Liam Cosgrave, the son of W. T. Cosgrave. When the 1973 election was called by Fianna Fáil, Fine Gael and Labour agreed to fight it as a coalition, and between them won an overall majority of seats. The party's strength in each region and even in each constituency, in so far as the 1969 revisions permit comparisons, changed very little over these three elections. In 1973 it was almost 6 percent stronger in the most agricultural areas than in the least agricultural ones. The passing of the leadership to Cosgrave, who sits for the wealthiest constituency in the country (Dún Laoghaire and Rathdown) seems to have had little effect upon the nature of the party's support. Its attainment of office does not seem to have harmed it in the poorest regions, as in three 1975 by-elections it did better in both Galway and Mayo than it had at the 1973 general election.

IV THE LABOUR PARTY

The outstanding feature of the Irish Labour Party, when viewed in a comparative perspective, has always been its weakness. Since 1922 it has never won as much as 18 percent of the votes cast, and has always trailed behind both Fianna Fáil and Fine Gael. Moreover, on three occasions 'minor' parties (the Farmers Party in 1923, the Centre Party in 1933 and Clann na Poblachta in 1948) have polled more strongly. Against its weakness must be set its persistence — it remains a political force, while parties which for a time burned more brightly have long departed from the scene.

Several explanations of Labour's failure to attain major party status have been offered. One cites the lack of a large industrial proletariat, but this merely raises the question of why the party has failed to capture the support of what industrial labour force exists. Farrell (1970) has contended persuasively that Labour's failure to contest the 1918 election, arguably the foundation of contemporary Irish politics, resulted in its being subsequently frozen out of the political system. It can be pointed out, however, that in the 1922 election Labour won as many votes as de Valera's anti-Treaty Sinn Féin and that the present apparently stable three-party system has existed only since 1965. Chubb (1964 : 213; 1974 : 58-60) makes the valid point that Labour is a class-based party operating in a political system which apparently lacks underlying cleavages. Several writers allude to the electoral system (the single transferable vote in multi-member constitutencies). Both O'Leary (1961 : 18) and Murply (1969 : 154) believe that STV, by enabling the party to win seats with only a limited amount of support, may have reduced its incentive to shake off its working-class image and seek to broaden its appeal and attract middle-class votes like the British Labour Party. Certainly the electoral system has protected Labour from the fate suffered by, say, the British Liberal Party, its share of the seats being on average only about 1 percent below its share of the votes (Gallagher, 1975 : 502).

In the early years after the state's foundation Labour tried without much success to divert the electorate's attention from the Treaty issue to socio-economic questions. It gave its support in the Dáil to Fianna Fáil after the 1932 and 1937 elections. It reached its nadir in 1933, when it won fewer than 6 percent of the votes, but its strength rose at each of the next three elections to about 16 percent in 1943. Seemingly significantly, its gains in Dublin City, where it had always been weak, were 6 percent higher than its gains in the rest of the country between 1938 and 1943. Its hopes of achieving a long-awaited breakthrough in the capital were dashed, however, when a deep-rooted conflict in the trade union movement came to a head. The giant Irish Transport and General Workers' Union left the Irish Trade Union Congress, and five of the eight Labour T.D.s belonging to the union broke away to form the National Labour Party (see Nevin, 1969) National Labour's allegations that the

ILP was controlled by Communists may have been as damaging as the split itself;[10] in any case the two squabbling wings did not appeal to wavering voters and between them they won 4 percent fewer votes in 1944 than Labour had won in 1943.

Both factions participated in the first Inter-Party government, and National Labour rejoined the ILP in 1950. Labour did not benefit from this first taste of office as much as Fine Gael did, however, as it appeared that 'Fine Gael (was) dictating policies in which Labour acquiesced in its hunger for office' (Viney and Edwards, 1969 : 90). While Fine Gael's vote rose by over a half between 1948 and 1961, Labour's strength remained at about 11 percent at every election between 1944 and 1961, except for a slight drop in 1957, after the unpopular second Inter-Party government.

In 1960 William Norton, who had led the party since 1932, retired and was succeeded by Brendan Corish, under whom Labour strengthened its post-1957 resolve to eschew further coalitions and to work for the formation of a Labour government. At first this stragety appeared to be succeeding — at the 1965 election its share of the votes rose and it won 22 seats, a figure previously equalled only in June 1927. In 1969 its number of votes rose to an all-time peak, but it lost four seats, partly because of a revision of constituency boundaries which favoured Fianna Fáil (see Gallagher, 1975 : 510-11). Labour and Fine Gael fought and won the 1973 election as a coalition, and Labour obtained five of the fifteen ministries in the government.

Ecological analysis of the party's support between 1927 and 1965 reveals it to have remained remarkably stable. The regression equations presented in Table 6 show a consistently strong and positive relationship between Labour's strength and the proportion of farm labourers in each area, and an equally strong but negative relationship with the proportion of farmers.

The proportion of farm labourers has been the strongest predictor of Labour's strength at a majority of the fourteen elections for which this analysis has been conducted; the simple correlation between the two variables has had an average value of 0.51, and it would seem that the widely-held view that the backbone of Labour's support over the years has been agricultural labourers is an accurate one.

There is no evidence, however, to sustain the opinion that farmers, even small farmers, have had much tendency to vote Labour. At every election the proportion of farmers has been strongly and negatively correlated with Labour's strength, and at elections up to 1948 the relationship with the proportion of farmers employing no labour, i.e. small

TABLE 6

Support of Labour Party, Related to Ecological Variables, at elections
1927-65

Election	Farm labourers	Farmers	R^2	F	Percentage vote
1927(1)	4.98 (13.94)***	-4.00 (9.00)**	0.52	11.53***	12.5
1927(2)	4.61 (12.86)***	-2.54 (3.86)*	0.44	8.37**	9.2
1932	2.68 (4.16)*	-2.89 (4.91)*	0.31	4.68*	7.9
1933	3.03 (5.78)**	-2.54 (3.95)*	0.32	5.02*	5.8
1937	4.76 (11.10)***	-4.76 (11.02)***	0.53	11.68***	10.3
1938	3.97 (11.33)***	-3.81 (10.71)***	0.53	11.65***	10.0
1943	4.65 (17.76)***	-3.60 (10.99)***	0.61	16.50***	15.7
1944	5.79 (17.78)***	-3.61 (7.10)**	0.57	14.16***	11.3
1948	2.39 (2.89)	-4.79 (11.85)**	0.45	8.87**	11.3
1951	3.85 (8.57)**	-5.55 (17.93)***	0.59	15.98***	11.4
1954	4.73 (11.65)***	-5.23 (14.15)***	0.65	19.76***	12.1
1957	5.12 (17.41)	-4.22 (11.91)***	0.58	15.69***	9.1
1961	6.58 (22.67)***	-4.11 (8.94)**	0.60	16.83***	11.6
1965	5.07 (17.75)***	-4.44 (13.92)***	0.61	16.88***	15.4

farmers, was even more strongly negative. Labour's failure to win votes from farmers is due mainly to its image as a working-class party with strong trade union links, and to periodic allegations that Labour would nationalize land holdings if elected. In truth Labour has made few genuine attempts to appeal to farmers, and such efforts as it has made have generally failed — in 1969 it put up a former President of the National Farmers' Association in North Tipperary, but he won only 517 votes and finished bottom of the poll.

In general Labour has been strongest in constituencies with high unemployment rates and a high ratio of farm labourers to farmers, and weakest where the proportion of the labour force in agriculture is high, where there is a high proprtion of Irish speakers and where the emigration rate is high. At the four elections for which the variable has been available, the proportion of dwellings which are council houses has been strongly correlated with the party's strength (average $r = 0.56$) — the 1969 Gallup survey found that council house tenants in every social class were more prone than home-owners to vote Labour (Whyte, 1974 : 633).

Labour, it is clear, has fared best in the wealthiest constituencies. Its strength has always been positively related to the rateable value of land and to the average income per worker, while in the poorest areas, characterized by high emigration rates, it has been weak. The negative relationship between the party's strength and the proportion of Irish speakers (average $r = -0.35$) may well be reflected at the individual level. Labour is the only major party with an English-language name, but more importantly its extra-insular outlook and affiliations — it has connections with the United Kingdom through the trade unions, and is also a member of the Socialist International — may make it suspect in the eyes of those working for an 'Irish Ireland', particularly since the Gaelic revival movement has traditionally been hostile to 'foreign' mores; 'the ban' on players of Gaelic games playing or attending non-Gaelic games, for example (see Coogan, 1966 : 202-5), was only recently repealed.

The outstanding feature of Labour's support is its stability; none of the simple correlations with any of the ecological variables has changed its value significantly over the period (Gallagher, 1974 : 88-90). Table 6 shows that the proportion of farm labourers has been significant at the 0.001 level at most elections. The close nature of the relationship is emphasized by the fact that the correlation of the two variables has been weakest at those three elections — 1932, 1933 and 1948 — at which Labour was weakest, suggesting that the party may have lost a certain amount of support among farm labourers at these elections, and it will be shown in section VI that there is other evidence to suggest that farm labourers withheld their votes from Labour in the early thirties.

A breakdown of Labour's strength by the strength of agriculture in constituencies also shows very little change since 1927. The party has always been weak in the most agricultural constituencies – only once, in 1943, has it won more than 10 percent of the votes here, and its average strength has been only 6.1 percent. In the 'intermediate' and least agricultural areas it has always been considerably stronger, and its share of the votes in each was similar up to 1961, averaging about 14 percent. Since 1961, Labour has made large advances in the least agricultural areas while its support elsewhere has fallen off.

Most striking has been the change in its position in Dublin (see Table 7). Labour was stronger outside Dublin than within the city at

TABLE 7
Breakdown of Labour's Strength at Elections 1961-73

	1961	1965	1969	1973
Dublin City	7.97	19.52	30.93	23.57
Other constituencies	12.32	14.53	14.12	11.64
All constituencies	11.65	15.38	17.02	13.67

all but two of the elections up to and including that of 1961, but in both 1969 and 1973 it was twice as strong in the capital as elsewhere. In the mid-1960s Labour moved to the Left, and took several steps designed to increase its appeal to industrial workers and Socialists in general. In 1965 it made gains in Dublin similar to those it had made in 1943, but this time the labour movement remained united and it went on to achieve startling success in 1969. It overtook Fine Gael within the city and was only 8 percent behind Fianna Fáil; in Dublin North-West David Thornley became the first Labour candidate ever to top the poll in a Dublin constituency, and in Dublin South-West the party created another precedent by winning a plurality of the votes. Eight of its T.D.s then sat for Dublin City, with another from the suburb of Dún Laoghaire, while its support outside the city fell slightly.

The 1973 election was a disappointment to the party. It fell back by 7 percent within Dublin, where it was once more overtaken by Fine Gael, and by 2 percent elsewhere. It also lost three of its Dublin seats while gaining four in the rest of the country. Nevertheless, it was still much stronger in Dublin than in most other areas. Its share of the votes in the capital was exceeded in only three constituencies (Limerick East,

Dublin County North and the Labour stronghold of Wexford) and 29 percent of its total votes were won in Dublin City, and it seems finally to have shaken off its traditional dependence upon farm labourers' votes.

V MINOR PARTIES AND INDEPENDENTS

Of the sixteen elections covered in this paper, only three — those of 1937, 1938 and 1969 — have involved only the major parties and Independents. Each of the others was contested by a least one other party; these parties should perhaps be described as 'ephemeral' rather than 'minor' since their important common characteristic is that none of them has survived.[11] In 1923, 1933 and 1948, indeed, one of these parties won more votes than labour.

Some minor parties — for example, Clann Eireann in June 1927, the Irish Workers' League in September 1927, and Coras na Poblachta and Ailtiri na hAiseirighe in 1943 — have never won a sufficient number of votes or fought in enough constituencies to make possible an ecological analysis of their support. For some others ecological analysis is possible for some elections but not for others — the National League, the Farmers Party, Clann na Talmhan and Clann na Poblachta all lost strength after early success.

The Farmers Party

The Farmers Party, the political wing of the Farmers Union, contested every election from 1922 to 1932. It put up only 15 candidates in 1922, 7 being elected, but went to the other extreme in 1923, when it offered 64 candidates and won 15 seats. Thereafter it declined gradually in strength, its number of T.D.s falling to 11 in June 1927, 6 in September 1927 and 3 in 1932, after which election it was disbanded. It consistently supported the Cosgrave government, and the relationship came close to being a coalition after the September 1927 election when the Farmers' leader was given a Parliamentary Secretaryship (Manning, 1972 : 94-95). Negotiations on a possible merger between the two parties had taken place earlier in 1927, and had been concluded to the satisfaction of the negotiators, but a majority of the Farmers rejected the idea (Moss, 1933 : 144-45).

The nucleus of the Farmers Party's support, it is generally agreed, was formed by relatively wealthy farmers (Chubb, 1974 : 83; Manning, 1972 : 95; O'Sullivan, 1940 : 182). Moreover, the party was dominated and controlled by them — all of its T.D.s were sizeable farmers.

Table 8 presents regression equations relating the party's support in 1927 to the proportion of farm labourers in each area; this variable was the most strongly related to the Farmers' support at these elections. It

TABLE 8

Farmers Party's support in 1927, Related to Proportion of Farm Labourers

Election	Farm labourers	R^2	F	Percentage vote
1927(1)	3.72 (11.77)**	0.35	11.77**	8.9
1927(2)	4.42 (16.67)***	0.43	16.67***	6.6

may be of course, that the relationship did not hold at the individual level, and it might be suggested that it derives solely from the fact that the presence of farm labourers implies the presence of large farmers who employed these labourers.

It would be unwise, however, to dismiss the observed relationship so summarily. It is not unreasonable to suppose that a number of farm labourers were attracted by a party fighting for the interests of large-scale farming, on the prosperity of which their employment depended, an attraction no doubt greater among non-unionized farm labourers who saw their interests and their employers' as identical than among the more class-conscious unionized farm workers who probably voted Labour. One of the Farmers' election advertisements was addressed to farm labourers, reading: 'If your Employers prosper you prosper. Support the Farmers Party, which has at heart the welfare of our common Industry.' There was also a marked relationship between the party' strength and the ratio of farm labourers to farmers ($r = 0.40$), emphasizing that the Farmers Party was strongest in the large farming areas.

Although there is, then, evidence that both the Farmers Party and Labour won votes from farm labourers, in other respects the parties' support bases were very different. Labour's support was negatively related to the proportion of farmers in each area, while the Famers' support was positively related ($r = 0.26$); Labour was strongest where the unemployment rate was high, but the Farmers' support was unrelated to unemployment.

The National League

The National League was formed in September 1926 by Captain William Redmond, son of the penultimate leader of the Irish Parliamentary Party. In June 1927 it won over 7 percent of the votes and eight seats, but in

August 1927 it joined with Labour and Fianna Fáil in an abortive attempt to defeat the government and in doing so probably signed it own death warrant. One of its T.D.s defected in professed disgust to Cumann na nGaedheal and another abstained, and the vote precipitated the September election, at which it 'received a mandate to leave politics'. It lost three-quarters of its votes and all but two of its seats, and dissolved itself in 1931.

Reliable scholarly writing on the party is extremely limited — indeed, the only original research seems to be that conducted over forty years ago by Moss. Although he describes it (1933 : 27) as 'a party of malcontents representing nothing fundamental in Irish political life' and maintains that its sole proposal was that W. T. Cosgrave and de Valera, along with their followers, should retire from politics, which would then be left to men who had taken no part in the Civil War (cf. O'Sullivan, 1940 : 184), he goes on to show that the party possessed a rather more coherent set of policies.

In early 1927 Redmond put forward a Bill for assisting the 'rent-burdened town tenants' (Moss, 1933 : 141-42) and in the June 1927 election the National League was supported by Town Tenants' Leagues in Dublin and Galway (ibid. : 149). In addition, modifications of the licensing laws proposed by the Justice Minister, Kevin O'Higgins, had alienated publicans, and the National League made a special appeal to them. Thirdly, it suggested that social relief should be given to the old and to British ex-servicemen (ibid. : 155). The latter in particular felt in need of a champion of their interests — having fought for Britain in the First World War with the encouragement of the Irish political elite of the time, by the early 1920s they found themselves stigmatized by their past membership of the 'oppressor's army'. Significantly, when an attempt was being made to persuade a National League T.D. to support the government in a crucial division, it was apparently put to him that 'the ex-Servicemen of Sligo had certainly never sent him to the Dáil for the purpose of putting Mr Cosgrave out of office' (O'Sullivan, 1940 : 220).[12]

Unfortunately none of these possibilities can be tested empirically by the use of existing data. Ecological analysis of the party's vote is not helpful because no strong relationships appear — the strongest was a positive correlation with the unemployment rate ($r = 0.30$), and the next strongest a negative one with the proportion of farmers ($r = -0.27$). Neither is sufficiently strong to enable firm conclusions to be drawn.

More than most parties, perhaps, the National League relied upon the ability of its candidates as individuals to attract voters. Its election organization was left to the candidates themselves (Moss, 1933 : 57), and its two most prominent figures, Captain Redmond and James Coburn, had large local personal followings.[13] The rather amorphous nature of the party was shown in the June election results, when it picked up lower transfers from different parties in different areas of the country (Moss, 1933 : 157-58), and during the debate on the no confidence motion when it was racked by internal conflict. Harsh as it was, Moss's judgement that it represented nothing fundamental seems justified by the party's failure to establish itself after its early success.

Sinn Féin

Sinn Féin contested only four elections in the period 1927 to 1973, those of June 1927, 1957, 1961, and 1973. Having beeing through what Pyne (1969 : 30) terms its Monarchist, Nationalist and Republican phases, Sinn Féin was by 1927 the name of an 'Extremist or Fundamentalist' party consisting of those who had refused to follow de Valera when in 1926 he began preparing the ground for eventual entry into the Dáil. Its members continue to deny the legitimacy of the 'British-imposed Free State Parliament', and neither its five successful candidates in June 1927 nor its four in 1957 took their seats.

Since Sinn Féin was unequivocally an abstentionist party, those who voted for it were explicitly endorsing its uncompromising attitude. Although Irish T.D.s are often expected to act as brokers between their constituents and central government — to 'go about persecuting civil servants' in Senator Michael Hayes's words (see Chubb, 1963) — the consideration of how adequately Sinn Féin candidates could fill this role was clearly absent. Sinn Féin's own assessment of its character was neatly summed up during the 1957 election campaign by one of its Dublin candidates, Tomás Ó Dubhghaill, who stated, 'Sinn Féin is not a political party; it is a national movement with a policy' (quoted in *Irish Times*, 23 February 1957).

In June 1927 Sinn Féin put up 15 candidates, 5 of whom were elected, and won nearly 4 percent of the votes cast. The party lacked the organization, the finances and the appeal of Fianna Fáil — most importantly, it no longer had de Valera at its head. Despite its abstentionism, the personal element was clearly a factor in its support — all but one of its candidates had been elected in 1923. Two of its T.D.s, Austin Stack and Oscar Traynor, had outstanding records in the 'national struggle' — Traynor later rose to high rank in Fianna Fáil — and another, Mrs Brugha, was the widow of a leading anti-Treatyite.

Despite this, it is possible to detect a socio-economic component in the party's support in June 1927 (see Table 9); the party tended to fare

TABLE 9

Sinn Féin's support, Related to Ecological Variables

Election	Farm labourers	Emigration rate	Non-Catholics	R^2	F	Percentage vote
1927(1)	-1.64 (7.37)	0.94 (2.06)	-1.15 (3.25)*	0.41	4.65*	3.6
1957	-1.87 (2.78)	2.72 (5.72)**		0.25	3.75*	5.3
1961	-1.09 (3.75)	1.27 (5.00)		0.26	3.82*	3.1

best in constituencies with a low proportion of farm labourers and of Protestants, and a high emigration rate. Its support was also correlated positively with the proportion of Irish speakers (r = 0.32). There was little relationship between Sinn Féin's strength and that of Fianna Fáil,[14] and whereas Fianna Fáil's strength was strongly related to the proportion of farmers in each area, there was no relationship between this variable and Sinn Féin's support. Unlike Fianna Fáil, Sinn Féin won above-average support in Dublin and Cork cities. However, although clearly there was some socio-economic basis to the party's support, the domination of Irish politics during the 1920s by the Treaty issue and by a handful of personalities of outstanding stature was such that the personal factor cannot be ignored. In the final resort the vote won by Sinn Féin in a particular constituency may have been determined primarily by the number, and calibre, of the incumbent T.D.s who remained with the party after de Valera left it in 1926.

Sinn Féin fought two by-elections in August 1927, but no further candidates stood on the Sinn Féin label until the 1957 general election. In 1956 the IRA started a fresh campaign of violence to end partition, and although Chubb (1959 : 183) describes the 1957 election as 'dull', O'Leary (1961 : 46, n. 120; 93) writes that it was 'waged in an atmosphere resembling that of 1933 and earlier' and refers to 'enormous demonstrations of sympathy' at the funerals of some IRA members killed in border action.

Capitalizing on the upsurge of support for 'republicanism', Sinn Fein put up 19 candidates, some of whom were then in jail, and had 4, all with close IRA connections, elected (Bell, 1972 : 358; Coogan, 1970 : 264, 272; Chubb, 1959 : 220). This was quite a creditable performance for an abstentionist party — in all it won over 5 percent of the votes, and an average of 11 percent in those constituencies it actually contested. It naturally did well in constituencies close to the border, but its best performance was in South Kerry and it won votes in every area of the country except the south-east. By 1961, however, the border campaign had come to seem sterile and futile, and in the election of that year Sinn Féin lost all of its seats and its votes fell from 66,000 to 36,000.

Although it had vaguely radical social policies, Sinn Féin made its appeal to the entire nation, on an issue (anti-partitionism) scarcely designed to appeal to anyone on material grounds. Consequently it could be expected that its strength would be only weakly correlated with socio-economic factors. As Table 9 shows, however, it was strongest in constituencies with high emigration rates, and tended to be weak where farm labourers were numerous, a pattern similar to the 1927 one although there was little similarity in geographical terms with the support of the 1927 party (see section VI). In both 1957 and 1961 Sinn Féin's support was correlated positively with the proportion of farmers in each area (r = 0.35 in 1957, 0.49 in 1961) and negatively with the average income per gainfully employed person (r = -0.37 in 1957, -0.53 in 1961).

The party was strongest in the most agricultural parts of the country; unlike Clann na Poblachta it was fairly weak in Dublin City. Although both Clann na Poblachta and Sinn Féin offered policies with socialist and republican features, the crucial difference is that Sinn Féin's radicalism was merely incidental. Clann na Poblachta appealed to socialists in 1948 by undertaking to enter the Dáil and to attempt to alter the status quo; Sinn Féin undertook not to enter the Dáil. A vote for Sinn Féin could not help promote socialist policies, and this is reflected in the sources of the party's support. Sinn Féin returned to a state of electoral dormancy until the 1973 general election, when it put up candidates in ten constituencies. All fared badly, however, and only one saved his deposit. The negligible support it received, just 1 percent of the total votes cast, does not warrant extended consideration.

The Centre Party

The Centre Party existed for less than a year. It was formed in October 1932, its most prominent founders being men who were already sitting in the Dáil, like James Dillon and Frank MacDermot. Its declared aims at its formation were to help farmers recover their prosperity, to attempt to heal the wounds of the Civil War, and to pursue a policy of friendliness towards Britain and Northern Ireland (Lyons, 1971 : 521-22; Manning, 1972 : 96-98; Moss, 1933 : 186). At the 1933 election it put forward 26 candidates, of whom 11 were elected, fighting on a platform of ending the Economic War by negotiating with Britain (Moss, 1933 : 193). In September 1933 it merged with Cumann na nGaedheal and the National Guard to form Fine Gael.

Little evidence is available concerning the sources of the party's support. Coogan (1966 : 77) suggests that it 'represented the interests of big farmers' and that 'to all intents and purposes (it) subsumed the old Farmers' Party'. O'Leary (1961 : 29) states that it 'drew support from Cumann na nGaedheal'. Certainly the two parties had a lot in common, principally opposition to the Economic War with the United Kingdom. A merger of the two parties was in the air in December 1932, and it was partly to forestall such an alliance that de Valera called the January 1933 election. The Centre Party's initial reservations about such a merger derived not from any feelings that the parties might prove incompatible, but the reverse — Centre Party leaders feared that the similarity of the parties might result in their party's simply being absorbed by the much larger Cumann na nGaedheal (Manning, 1970 : 98; Moss, 1933 : 191-92). Frank MacDermot, indeed, opposed the merger, feeling that the Centre Party could eventually have grown to the strength necessary to form a government had it remained a separate party (see interview in *Irish Times*, 8 April 1961).

The result of an ecological analysis of the Centre Party's support at the 1933 election is shown in Table 10 below. The ecological variable to which

TABLE 10

Support of Centre Party in 1933, Related to Ecological Variables

Election	Farm labourers	Farmers	Irish speakers	R^2	F	Percentage vote
1933	3.12 (5.03)**	2.59 (3.46)*	-2.82 (3.41)	0.44	5.17**	9.1

its strength was most strongly related is the proportion of farm labourers. It was argued earlier that the Farmers Party (whose pattern of support was similar to the Centre Party's) may have won votes from farm labourers, and there is even more reason to suppose that the Centre Party did so. Labour, which usually relied upon farm labourers' support (see section IV), won its lowest-ever share of the votes (5.8 percent) in 1933. Since the 1932 election Labour had supported the Fianna Fáil minority government, and the Economic War which followed the latter's refusal to hand over the Land Annuity payments had hurt particularly the wealthier farming areas, which had previously exported much of their produce to Britain. This analysis suggests that a number of farm labourers voted for the Centre Party in 1933 in the belief that it would try to end the Economic War and thus help restore the prosperity of the large-scale farming areas.

For the same reason, it may well be that there was some tendency among farmers, especially larger farmers, to vote for Centre Party candidates, although for many farmers the impetus given in this direction by economic self-interest would have been countered by Fianna Fáil's appeal to their nationalism. The negative relationship between the party's support and the proportion of Irish speakers in each area supports this contention, and it would not be surprising if it were reflected at the individual level. The Centre Party, after all, appeared to be the least republican of all the parties, and many spoke of it as a new party 'which would bring under one banner all those in favour of improved relations with Britain' (Lyons, 1971 : 522). The 'West Briton' outlook of some of its leaders would hardly recommend it to the most ardent protagonists of an 'Irish Ireland'.

From which party or parties did the Centre Party win votes? Correlation of its share of the votes in each constituency with the Farmers Party's vote in the previous three elections produces high positive coefficients (see section VI), which tends to bear out Coogan's view that the Centre Party largely inherited the Farmers' votes. A correlation of the party's strength in 1933 with the losses of other parties between 1932 and 1933 shows that its gains were correlated positively with the losses of Cumann na nGaedheal ($r = 0.34$), Independents ($r = 0.28$) and the Farmers Party ($r = 0.35$),[15] but were pratically unrelated to Labour's losses.

There is, then, some evidence to suggest that the Centre Party drew votes from Cumann na nGaedheal and that it picked up some of the old Farmers Party's support. However, the period 1932 to 1933 was one of political upheaval and, if Independents are included, a five-party system existed at each election. It must be assumed that there was a good deal of cross-switching among voters which would not show up in aggregate returns.

Clann na Talmhan

Clann na Talmhan — the name means 'Family of the Soil' — was formed in August 1938. It performed well at the first election it contested, in 1943, winning 15 seats and 11 percent of the votes, and more or less maintained its strength at the 1944 election. It fell to 6 percent of the votes in 1948 and dwindled steadily thereafter, and although it had candidates returned at every election until 1965 no ecological analysis of its support has been carried out for elections after 1948.[16]

It is generally agreed that Clann na Talmhan was a small farmers' party and drew most of its support from them (Chubb, 1974 : 87; Lysaght, 1970 : 116-18, 151-52; Manning, 1972 : 99-101; Murphy, 1975 : 115; Rumpf, 1959 : 167), although one writer (Coogan, 1966 : 90) maintains that it represented the interests of larger farmers.

Table 11 confirms that Clann na Talmhan's support rested largely

TABLE 11

Support of Clann na Talmhan, Related to Ecological Variables, at Elections 1943-48

Election	Farmers	Non-Catholics	R^2	F	Percentage vote
1943	5.46 (10.46)***	-2.39 (1.93)	0.39	6.65**	11.3
1944	5.08 (6.95)**	-4.29 (4.80)*	0.38	6.45**	10.8
1948	4.32 (14.08)	-2.93 (6.45)	0.51	11.43***	5.6

upon farmers, although it polled relatively weakly in constituencies with a high proportion of Protestants. In addition its support at each election was correlated strongly and negatively with the ratio of farm labourers to farmers, and every strongly and positively with the proportion of farmers who employed no labour, showing that the party was strongest where farm size was small and where few farmers were wealthy enough to employ labourers — its image as a small farmers' party seems to be borne out.

There can be little doubt that in 1943 Clann na Talmhan won the votes of former supporters of both Fianna Fáil and Fine Gael. The losses of each party between 1938 and 1943, as we have shown, were strongly correlated with Clann na Talmhan's gains, and the mean two-party swing from each to Clann na Talmhan, in constitutencies where that party stood, was about 13 percent. In the most agricultural areas of the country Clann na Talmhan's strength in 1943 was 22.15 percent, while between 1938 and 1943 Fianna Fáil's share of the votes here fell by 18 percent and Fine

Gael's by 13 percent.

This shows emphatically that Clann na Talmhan's emergence reflected a dissatisfaction in the poorest areas of the country not just with Fianna Fáil but with the whole party system as it then existed. The small farmers of the depressed regions clearly felt that none of the established parties was concerned to safeguard their interests and that these could be pressed only by a party of their own.

Consequently Clann na Talmhan acted mainly as a parliamentary pressure group on behalf of its supporters; it never had major party aspirations and never sought even to represent the whole of the agricultural community. Its decline can be attributed partly to its general lack of effectiveness, but mainly to the revival of agriculture after 1948, and particularly to the obvious importance attached by the Inter-Party governments to the alleviation of the problems of the small farmers of Ireland's poorest regions.

Clann na Poblachta

Clann na Poblachta was formed in July 1946; it first contested a general election in 1948, and last stood in 1965, the year in which it wound itself up. Its electoral record was one of steady decline, and the 1954 election is the last for which its support has been analysed in this paper. Whereas in 1954 it stood in 17 constituencies, winning 3 seats and nearly 4 percent of the votes, in 1957 it fought only 12 constituencies and won 1.7 percent of the votes and just 1 seat, even its leader failing to gain re-election.

Unlike Clann na Talmhan the party did not aim to act purely as a pressure group. In 1948 some of its candidates seemed to envisage a Clann na Poblachta government (O'Leary, 1961 : 41) and its candidature patterns show that the party seriously believed that it could win enough seats to form a government, for it offered 93 candidates (at least two in every constituency except Cork South) for the 147 seats at stake. It offered new policies in several fields, as befitted a party hoping to win strong support from most sections of the community. One of its main proposals was the introduction of some of the welfare state facilities then being promoted in the United Kingdom by the Labour government, such as guaranteed wage rates and better social services. In addition, and somewhat inconsistently for a party aiming 'to get away from the *damnosa hereditas* of the Civil War' (O'Leary, 1961 : 40), it advocated a stronger anti-partitionist line with the aim of bringing about a 32-county Republic.

The party, then, made its appeal to two distinct groups, to socialists and social democrats who, for one reason or another, were ready to vote for a party other than Labour, and to die-hard republicans who had become convinced that Fianna Fáil was paying only lip-service to the idea of winning back the north.[17] If it won support from both of these groups it would be difficult to identify its bases of support in terms of social groups. Republicanism and socialism have generally been mutually antagonistic rather than complementary forces in Ireland's history, and in the 1930s the IRA resisted attempts by some of its members to transform it into a socialist and republican movement (see Coogan, 1970 : 77-83; Bell, 1972 : 132-41). The weakness, almost absence, of a socialist-republican tradition makes it reasonable to suppose that Clann na Poblachta had the support of 'socialists' in some areas and of 'republicans' in others, rather than of 'republican socialists' in all areas. While it may be assumed that its socialist supporters came predominantly from areas where the Labour Party was strongest, i.e. from relatively industrial areas where such agriculture as was carried out involved a high proportion of farm labourers, republican parties — Fianna Fáil in its early days and Sinn Féin in 1957 and 1961 — have won most votes in heavily agricultural regions. If this is the case, the different characteristics of the party's two support bases would act against each other in an ecological analysis, to give the impression that its support was not strongly related to any of the census variables.

Table 12 provides some confirmation of this. In 1948 Clann na

TABLE 12

Support of Clann na Poblachta, Related to Ecological Variables, at Elections 1948-54

Election	Emigration rate	Farmers	R^2	F	Percentage vote
1948	-1.23 (1.92)		0.08	1.92	13.2
1951		2.23 (6.22)	0.20	6.22*	4.1
1954		2.56 (8.60)**	0.30	8.60**	3.8

Poblachta was relatively strong in constituencies with a low emigration rate, but the relationship is not very strong. The party's support is related only weakly to each of the ecological variables, and none of the simple correlation coefficients has an absolute value greater than 0.3. Its strength was related negatively to the proportion of the labour force in agriculture (r = -0.20) and to the proportion of farm labourers (r = -0.13), and positively to the rateable value of land (r = 0.23) and to the proportion of Irish speakers (r = 0.23).

However, the weakness of these correlations cannot be attributed to an even spread of Clann na Poblachta's strength across the country — its share of the votes ranged from 4.6 percent in Laoghis-Offaly to 26.4 percent in Dublin South-West. Its support in 1948 was 'twin-peaked'; as would be expected it was strong in both the most and the least agricultural constituencies, where it won 14.2 and 15.6 percent of the votes, respectively, and the 'valley' of its support lay in the intermediate constitutencies (10.1 percent). It was especially strong in Dublin City, where it took 19 percent of the votes.

Between 1948 and 1951 it lost votes in every constitutency except Cavan, but its losses were heaviest in the least agricultural areas, especially in Dublin, where two of its former T.D.s left the party and were re-elected as Independents, and where its strength slumped to 4 percent.

Clann na Poblachta lost votes most heavily in the least agricultural regions because between 1948 and 1951 it alienated its socialist supporters more than its republican ones. When, early in 1951, the 'Mother and Child' scheme, under which the state would have given free medical assistance to mothers and children without a means test, proved unacceptable to the Catholic hierarchy, it was the party's leader, Seán MacBride, who took the initiative in dismissing the Clann na Poblachta Minister who had been responsible for the scheme, Dr Noel Browne (see Whyte, 1971 : ch. 7 and 8 and Appendices A and B). This apparent readiness to sacrifice the party's social policies in order to retain its government posts led to the defection of Browne, McQuillan and several other leading members and also, it may be supposed, of many of those who had voted for it in 1948 because they were attracted by its stance on socio-economic issues. On the other hand, although nothing the party had done had brought a united Ireland any nearer, it had at least been part of a government which, as Coogan (1966 : 97) says, '(gave) the republicans their Republic'.

In both 1951 and 1954 Clann na Poblachta was strongest in the most agricultural regions; its strength was strongly correlated with the proportion of farmers and, in contrast to 1948, it was strongest in areas of high emigration. At each of these elections its support came mainly from those regions which have traditionally given most support to republican parties. Betweeen 1951 and 1954 its strength in Dublin actually rose slightly, to 6.7 percent; this minor revival was due to a swing away from

Fianna Fáil to the parties which had made up the first Inter-party government, and it seems that only in Dublin was the party still sufficiently well organized to take advanatage of this.

As far as it is possible to tell — the 1947 boundary revisions make direct comparisons between constituencies impossible — it seems that in 1948 Clann na Poblachta won votes which in 1944 had gone to Fianna Fáil or Clann na Talmhan; between the two elections Fianna Fáil lost 7 percent of the votes and Clann na Talmhan lost 6 percent, while Clann na Poblachta gained 13 percent and the strength of the other parties and Independents altered little.

Independents

Independent deputies were a powerful bloc in Irish politics for the first forty years of the state's existence, usually winning more seats than Labour and occasionally providing crucial Dáil support for governments. Chubb (1957 : 134-35) describes several categories of Independent: there have been those standing on no platform other than representation of local interests, former Unionists or nationalists in the old Irish Parliamentary Party tradition, Independent Farmers, sometimes supported by county Farmers' Associations, their urban counterparts the 'Business Candidates', and rebels from one of the established parties.

Independents have been helped in the past by the strength of localism and the importance of personal contact in Irish politics. Irish deputies, especially in rural areas, are regarded by many of their constituents as brokers between themselves and the state, and some voters believe that a T.D.'s intervention is necessary to obtain even straightforward social service benfits like pensions, a belief some T.D.s encourage.[18] In consequence (Chubb, 1957 : 132)

> The Deputy who works hard to forward the personal interests of his constituents and to get, or seem to get, as much public money as possible for his area is virtually assured of re-election. He does not *have* to be a party man to do this. In circumstances such as these, Independents might . . . once in, continue to be returned regularly.

In recent years Independents' strength has slumped. In 1961 there were six Independent and five minor party T.D.s, but in 1965 there were only two of the former and one of the latter. In 1969 there was just one T.D. outside the three major parties, and in 1973 he was joined by an exile from Fianna Fáil. Since the 1948 election only seven Independents have been elected for the first time, and no new Independent has been elected since 1961. The difficulties now faced by aspiring Independent T.D.s are illustrated by the rout at the 1973 election of those who had resigned or been expelled from Fianna Fáil in 1970. Only Neil Blaney in North-East Donegal, where his personal 'machine' possesses formidable power, secured re-election. In South County Dublin a former senior minister lost his deposit, and in Wicklow a former parliamentary secretary, who had easily topped the poll at every election since 1957, was only just spared this ignominy.

It seems that the importance of a party label is increasing. Electioneering has become more expensive and more difficult for a candidate with no backing. The impact of the mass media, particularly television, may have caused the electorate to perceive elections increasingly in terms of national rather than local issues. It has been suggested that the steady reduction in the number of large constituencies may have militated against Independent candidates since small constituencies tend to produce greater disproportionality, but the evidence is that if the constituency revisions have been at all responsible for Independents' decline it has been by adversely affecting their ability to win votes rather than by making it hārder for them to win seats from a given number of votes (Gallagher, 1975 : 506).

Although Independent candidates have not formed a homogeneous group, it is reasonable to ask whether their support has come particularly from any one section of society. Table 13 shows a consistently strong relationship from 1927 to 1957 between Independents' strength and the proportion of non-Catholics in each area of analysis. At practically every election during the period this variable was the strongest predictor of Independents' support, and the average simple correlation coefficient was 0.53. While making all due allowance for the possibility that the relationship at the macro level differs from that at the micro level, it seems fair to conclude that Protestant voters have had a greater tendency than Catholics to vote for Independents.

At every election Independents' strength was negatively related to the proportion of farm labourers, sometimes strongly so. The relationships with most of the other ecological variables were generally weak, although at the 1948 election and during the 1950s the evidence suggests that, as Clann na Talmhan broke up, some of the farming vote went to Independents. Indeed, at these elections a number of Independents described themselves as 'Independent Farmers', and some were supported by county Farmers' Associations (cf. Chubb, 1957 : 134).

It was anticipated in 1922 when the Free State Constitution was framed that Protestants and ex-Unionists would continue for some years to vote for their own candidates, and it was partly to reassure them that

TABLE 13

Independents' support, Related to Ecological Variables, at elections
1927-65

Election	Non-Catholics	Farm labourers	Farmers	R^2	F
1927(1)	6.14 (7.96)**	-1.89 (0.74)		0.30	4.53*
1927(2)	5.99 (14.21)	-2.02 (1.89)		0.45	9.36**
1932	7.40 (22.18)***	-1.80 (1.34)		0.54	12.22***
1933	4.88 (14.42)***	-2.16 (2.75)		0.46	9.08**
1937	5.20 (17.66)	-3.97 (10.07)***		0.58	14.58***
1938	5.97 (32.18)***	-1.99 (3.66)*		0.64	18.52***
1943	3.25 (2.94)	-3.06 (2.47)		0.21	2.77
1944	4.28 (3.72)*	-4.51 (4.18)*		0.28	4.04*
1948	4.27 (5.72)**		3.40 (3.71)*	0.28	4.27*
1951	4.18 (7.16)**		2.94 (3.51)*	0.32	5.06*
1954	3.53 (11.42)***		4.10 (15.05)***	0.55	12.87***
1957	2.79 (5.36)*		2.52 (4.27)*	0.28	4.29*
1961	0.09 (0.03)	-2.06 (5.80)**		0.12	2.13
1965	-0.76 (0.72)	-0.40 (0.21)		0.06	0.65

they would be represented in the Dáil in rough proportion to their strength that an electoral system with strong elements of P.R. was specified (O'Leary, 1961 : 12-13). In fact no 'ex-Unionist Party' was formed, although there was a sizeable and fairly cohesive group of Protestants in the Senate until it was abolished in 1937.

Although most ex-Unionist politicians prudently left Irish politics after 1922, this analysis suggests that Protestant voters tended to cast votes for Independents up to 1957. There is some evidence that Protestant voters still vote en bloc: Sacks (1970) reports that when Fine Gael put up a Protestant as one of their candidates in Donegal North East at the 1969 election, many Protestant voters switched from Fianna Fáil to Fine Gael.[19]

Table 14 shows the strength of Independents since 1927 in the four

TABLE 14

Breakdown of Independents' Strength at Elections 1927-73

Election	Most Protestant constituencies	Other constituencies	All constituencies
1927(1)	25.76	12.37	14.02
1927(2)	21.64	6.14	8.06
1932	26.54	8.18	10.46
1933	14.72	3.63	4.97
1937	18.64	8.47	9.70
1938	19.04	3.05	4.72
1943	13.73	7.29	8.03
1944	18.76	7.38	8.49
1948	17.92	7.03	8.27
1951	16.20	8.73	9.58
1954	13.31	4.74	5.68
1957	12.76	5.80	6.55
1961	2.70	6.13	5.77
1965	0	2.38	2.11
1969	4.90*	3.02	3.22
1973	10.92*	2.01	2.95

*Including the Donegal-Leitrim constituency.

most Protestant counties.[20] They were clearly much stronger in the most Protestant constituencies than elsewhere until 1961, in 1938 being six times stronger.[21] There is no reason to suppose that the Independents in Wicklow were supported particularly by Protestants, but a solid Protestant vote has undoubtedly existed in the three Ulster counties.

Certain candidates there — Major Sproule Myles and William Sheldon in Donegal, the Hasletts, Arthur Montgomery and Robert Houston in Monaghan and J. J. Cole in Cavan — were nominated by their respective County Protestant Associations, often held their election meetings in halls of the Orange Order, and won votes on the basis of being 'Protestant Independents' (cf. Sacks, 1970 : 535-36; Chubb, 1974 : 87; Gwynn, 1928 : 145-46).

To some extent changes in the major parties helped them win these votes from 1961 onwards; between 1957 and 1961 some of the most prominent politicians of the post-independence era, devout Catholics and veteran nationalists like de Valera and Mulcahy, retired from active politics. Although no doubt this made the major parties seem more acceptable to the Protestant community, another imporant factor was the 1961 Electoral (Amendment) Act, under which constituency boundaries were revised. The number of seats in Cavan was reduced from four to three; the quota rose by over 800 votes, and no Independent stood there in 1961. A detailed study of Donegal has been made by Sacks, who reports (1970 : 535-36):

> Prior to 1961 there were sufficient Protestants in Donegal to return 'one of their own' to the Dáil . . . But after (the 1961 Electoral Act) the situation changed substantially. The 1961 constituency revisions reduced the number of Protestants in the North-East to less than a Dáil quota. Protestant candidates, *per se,* could no longer be elected to parliament . . . After 1961, Fianna Fáil and Fine Gael made considerable progress in absorbing the 'Unionist' vote.

William Sheldon, the former Protestant Independent T.D. for Donegal, was given a seat in the Senate by the Taoiseach, as was J.J. Cole of Cavan.

Which party picked up the votes after 1961 which had previously gone, in Ulster, to Independents? Table 15 shows that both Fianna Fáil and Fine

TABLE 15

Breakdown of changes in percentage votes of parties between 1957 and 1961 Elections[22]

	FF	FG	Lab	Inds
Ulster	+3.72	+10.00	0	-12.86
Rest of Ireland	-5.28	+4.96	+2.75	+0.39
All constituencies	-4.50	+5.39	+2.54	+0.20

Gael fared much better in these constituencies in 1961 than they did in the rest of the country but, unless there was a good deal of concealed movement of voters, it must be concluded that Fine Gael won most of the votes which had previously gone to Independents. Although Sacks (1970 : 536) concludes that 'it was generally estimated in 1969 that the Protestant vote (in Donegal) was effectively divided between Fianna Fáil and Fine Gael at a ratio of two to one', the electoral returns show that between 1957 and 1961 in Donegal, Independents' share of the vote fell by 17 percent. while Fianna Fáil's rose by 2 percent, Fine Gael's by 11 percent and Sinn Féin's by 4 percent. The major parties shares of the votes remained close to their 1961 levels in both the 1965 and 1969 elections. there appears to be a certain conflict of evidence.

It is difficult to say which of these two parties might seem more attractive to Protestants. Fianna Fáil has always had less sympathy with the Protestants of Northern Ireland, but Fine Gael has appeared more concerned not to support any initative to which the Catholic hierarchy might object, an image strengthened by the Mother and Child affair and its aftermath.

VI THE PERSISTENCE OF PARTY SUPPORT 1927-73

Sections II-V of this paper have traced changes in the bases of the parties' support in terms of the ecological characteristics of constituencies. In this section we shall examine the persistence of their support in purely geographical terms.

The method used will be to correlate the parties' support in each of a number of areas of the country for all pairs of elections between a party's support at two elections indicates that its relative strengths in areas across the country were similar at the two elections; a low correlation indicates a change in the bases of the party' support. Since the correlations measure persistence in the geographical distribution of the parties' strength, they are not affected by changes in their absolute strength.

Successive revisions of constituency boundaries have reduced the number of areas for which direct comparisons over the entire period are possible. Between June 1927 and 1965 we have electoral data for 22 areas for each election.[23] Once again the 1969 Electoral Act has prevented the analysis being extended to the 1969 and 1973 elections — over the period 1927-73 only ten areas have retained the same boundaries, and of these one comprises ten counties and another six counties.[24]

Clearly in any country a certain amount of change from election to election is almost inevitable if only because of random factors and demographic changes. A major determinant of the extent of change will be the nature of the policies offered by the various parties, and their ability to retain their traditional supporters and attract new ones. Another determinant will be changes in the candidates they offer — a retiring Member of Parliament may have built up a sizeable personal vote which will not necessarily be transferred along with the purely party vote to this nominated successor.

It may be that in the Irish Republic this second factor is more important than in most other countries, since T.D.s are believed to derive much of their support from their perceived ability to extract from central government benefits for their area. Of the 197 respondents to a 1966 survey, fully 33 percent stated that the personality of a candidate was more important than his party affiliation in determining the destination of their first preference vote (Hart, 1970 : 390). The electoral system, providing as it does for multi-member constituencies, increases the importance of this factor. Candidates of one party are competing against each other as well as against candidates of other parties: 'a candidate cannot fight his fellow candidate on policy; he tries to seem a more assiduous and successful servant of his constituents' (Chubb, 1974 : 154). A more ambitious analysis than is being performed here would attempt to assess separately the effects of retiring incumbent deputies and the other components of this factor.

Table 16 shows that the pattern of Fianna Fáil's support is unlike that of the major parties in either Britain or the USA. Whereas the Conservatives' support at each pair of consecutive elections was correlated at a level of at least 0.90, the figure for Fianna Fáil has never reached that level. On the other hand, whereas the Democrats' correlations have generally been very high but have sometimes had extremely low values, indicating what Pomper calls a 'realigning' or a 'deviant' election when the party's geographical support base changes markedly,[25] none of the Fianna Fáil correlations is weaker than 0.53.

Clearly the elections of 1943 and 1951 come nearest to being realigning elections as far as Fianna Fáil is concerned, since its support at each was not strongly correlated with its support at the proceding election. As section II showed, at the 1943 election Fianna Fáil sustained heavy losses in its former strongholds, and in 1951 it made large gains in the least agricultural areas of the country but negligible gains in the most agricultural ones.

Examination of the full correlation matrix shows that three distinct phases have existed in the spatial distribution of Fianna Fáil's strength. The first phase lasted from June 1927 to 1938 — the correlations between

TABLE 16

Correlations Between Spatial Distribution of Fianna Fáil's Strength at Elections 1927-65

	Sept 1927	1932	1933	1937	1938	1943	1944	1948	1951	1954	1957	1961	1965
1927(1)	0.64	0.69	0.78	0.73	0.77	0.49	0.58	0.65	0.22	0.54	0.26	0.35	0.25
1927		0.83	0.85	0.65	0.79	0.31	0.37	0.47	-0.09	0.37	0.07	0.01	0.04
1932			0.87	0.64	0.81	0.25	0.39	0.59	-0.02	0.47	0.06	0.01	-0.05
1933				0.76	0.93	0.43	0.56	0.66	0.06	0.46	0.01	0.20	0.11
1937					0.87	0.62	0.70	0.66	0.29	0.56	0.23	0.37	0.26
1938						0.55	0.59	0.58	0.07	0.44	0.06	0.18	0.15
1943							0.85	0.61	0.58	0.54	0.48	0.57	0.55
1944								0.78	0.58	0.62	0.41	0.65	0.52
1948									0.53	0.79	0.48	0.62	0.44
1951										0.73	0.72	0.81	0.83
1954											0.79	0.71	0.67
1957												0.63	0.73
1961													0.82

pairs of elections in this period have a minimum value of 0.64. The second phase covers the three elections of 1943, 1944 and 1948 — in the small matrix formed by these elections the weakest correlation is 0.61, and in the third phase, from 1951 to 1965, the minimum was 0.63. The existence of these phases is illustrated by considering how the party's support at each election correlates with its support at the 1965 election — the correlations with the 1927-38 elections are weak, those with the 1943-48 elections are moderately strong, and there are high correlations between 1965 and the 1951-61 elections. The third phase clearly marked a further shift away from the pattern of the first rather than a reversion to it.

Examination of the corresponding matrix for Fine Gael (see Gallagher, 1974 : 152) reveals a low degree of persistence in its support; Cumann na nGaedheal's support also is not strongly related to the support won by Fine Gael at any election. Although the correlations between successive elections are generally weak, there have been no extremely low values apart from that of 0.09 between Cumann na nGaedheal's strength in 1933 and Fine Gael's in 1937.

However, it is not possible to detect the presence of deviant or realigning elections or distinct phases in the party's support. In general there were no dramatic changes from one pattern of support to another, but neither was there a high degree of persistence. The exception was the 1965 election; the party's support then was practically unrelated to its support at any previous election except that of 1961, and was correlated negatively as often as positively with its support at earlier elections. This change in 1965 was considered in section III, and since, as far as can be told, its new pattern of support persisted in 1969 and 1973, 1965 can be regarded as a realigning election for Fine Gael.

The geographical distribution of Labour's strength has varied much less than the two larger parties'. There has been a high degree of persistence between pairs of consecutive elections, the weakest correlation being 0.78, and it would obviously be pointless to seek deviant or realigning elections — regardless of alterations in the overall level of the party's support, its relative strength in the different areas has scarcely altered from election to election. Such change as has occurred has been cumulative, however, and the correlations between pairs of elections distant in time are not very strong. Even so, the lowest correlation in the matrix is 0.37 (cf. minima of -0.09 and -0.22 for Fianna Fáil and Fine Gael, respectively).

The pattern for the Irish Labour Party, then, bears considerable resemblance to those for the major British parties, and little resemblance to those for Fianna Fáil and Fine Gael. This may be because the ILP, like the British parties, can be regarded as a class-based party with an identifiable ideological outlook. It may well be that more Labour supporters vote for party rather than candidate than do supporters of the other major Irish parties. If this is the case, we should expect to find more persistence in Labour's support bases than in those of Fianna Fáil and Fine Gael, whose support would tend to fluctuate more from election to election as popular deputies retire and new candidates are offered in their stead.

There has been, then, a high degree of persistence in Labour's support — by and large its strongholds in the 1920s and 1930s were still its strongholds in the 1950s and 1960s, and its weakest areas also remained the same. Moreover in section IV it was shown that the social bases of its support changed little over the period.

These findings do not bear out the opinion, sometimes expressed that Labour's support has rested more upon the appeal of its candidates than on the appeal of the party itself. They also show that the party did not succeed in broadening its appeal between 1927 and 1965; it will be recalled (see section IV) that two authorities suggested that the P.R. electoral system had reduced the party's incentive to do so. However, they cannot tell us how vigorous have been the party's attempts to attract voters in its weak areas, and it seems more reasonable to attribute its perpetual weakness in certain areas to the paucity there of those social groups from whom it might be expected to draw support.

Independents are a heterogeneous group who have stood for various interests and sometimes for none, though it was shown in section V that their support has by no means come randomly from all sections of the electorate. Their support bases have remained more stable than might be expected, at least up to and including the 1957 election. Over the period 1927-57, indeed, Independents' support shows more continuity than either Fianna Fáil's or Fine Gael's, and almost as much as Labour's, a finding which well illustrates the volatility of the support of the largest two parties in this period.

However, Independents' strength fell sharply between 1957 and 1965, and the spatial distribution of their support in 1961 and 1965 bears little relation to their support at previous elections. Since this was a period of decline for Independents, this signified not that their support bases were shifting but that their former strongholds were crumbling.

Since such a disparate set of parties comes under the heading 'minor parties', it may seem meaningless to speak of the 'persistence' of their support, particularly since the parties themselves have not persisted. Nevertheless, correlation of their votes can show whether or not some of them have drawn their strongest support from the same areas of the country.

In fact, with two exceptions, the minor parties have had very different support bases There are high correlations ($r = 0.7$) between the Farmers Party's support in the two elections of 1927 and the Centre Party's support in 1933, which adds weight to the belief that the Centre Party inherited much of the Farmers' support. In addition, there are moderately high correlations ($r = 0.5$) between Clann na Poblachta's suppport in 1951 and 1954 and Sinn Féin's support in 1957 — these correlations are as strong as those between the Clann's support in 1948 and its support in 1951 and 1954 — which again is not surprising given the similarity, at these elections, of the two parties. It is also noticeable that Sinn Féin's support in 1957 and 1961 is quite unrelated ($r = 0.2$) to the support won in June 1927 by the party of the same name.

How unusual is the Irish pattern? Table 17 shows figures for Ireland and

TABLE 17

Correlations Between Spatial Distribution of Parties' Support at (a) Consecutive Elections (b) All Pairs of Elections

		(a) Mean coefficient	(b) Mean coefficient
Ireland	Fianna Fáil	0.75	0.49
	Fine Gael	0.66	0.38
	Labour	0.88	0.73
	Independents	0.67	0.44
Canada	Conservatives	0.79	0.57
	Liberals	0.89	0.79
United Kingdom	Conservatives	0.90	0.86
	Labour	0.96	0.93
	Liberals	0.75	0.58
United States	Democrats	0.77	0.46

Sources: **Canada:** Mackie (1971: Appendix 3). Period: 1949-68. No of elections: 8. No. of cases at each election: 12.
United Kingdom: Gallagher (1974: 135). Period: 1950-70. No. of elections: 7. No of cases at each election: 618.
United States: Pomper (1967: 545). Period: 1924-64. No. of elections: 11. No of cases at each election; presumably 50.

other countries for which comparable data are available, and makes it obvious that the two major Irish parties' support has tended to vary more between consecutive elections than has the support of all the British parties, both the Italian parties and the Canadian Liberals.

When the average correlations between all pairs of elections are considered, the situation becomes even more clear. Only the Irish Labour Party's support shows as much continuity as that of the major parties in Britain and Italy and the Canadian Liberals. Even the British Liberal Party, which had little organization in many parts of the country and whose strength has varied considerably over the period – it stood in 475 seats in 1950 and only 109 in 1951 – shows more persistence than Fianna Fáil or Fine Gael. The only party whose support has varied as much as the two major Irish parties: is the Democratic Party, and even the Democrats' low figure gives a somewhat false impression because of the fundamental change in their support at the 1960 and 1964 elections – the mean correlation for the period 1924 to 1956 was 0.80. It can only be concluded that, as far as can be told from the limited set of comparable data available, the geographical sources of the support of Fianna Fáil and Fine Gael have shown an unusually low degree of persistence.

VII CONCLUSION

Support for Irish political parties has rested upon clearer social and economic bases than some observers have suggested, although these have generally been less distinct than those underlying the support of parties in most Western democracies. In other respects, however, the Irish political party system's image of uniqueness seems to be borne out. There has been much less stability. in the support of the two major parties than in the support of major parties elsewhere (cf. Table 17).

In Ireland, realignments of the party system cannot be held to account for very much of the lack of persistence in the parties' support. Only the 1943 election, when the two major parties were shown to have lost the support of many small farmers, and the 1965 election, at which Fine Gael presented a new image, can be regarded as realigning elections.

The generally low level of persistence in the major parties' support indicates a lack of stability in the voting behaviour of the Irish electorate. Conceivably the youth of the polity, and consequently of the parties and the political system itself, has prevented electors settling down to stable voting habits; if this is the case, increasing stability can be expected in the future as the parties free themselves of their origins and come to bear more resemblance to parties in other West European democracies.

[70]

It may well be, on the other hand, that the instability observed for the past fifty years has derived from more fundamental characteristics of the Irish political system which set it apart from those of other countries, characteristics themselves deriving from the small size of the state, its basically rural nature, and perhaps the multi-member constituenices provided for by the constitution. If it is true that Irish voters wish their parliamentary representatives to act primarily as brokers between themselves and central and local government rather than as legislators or even lobby fodder, there seems no reason to expect increasing stability in the parties' support to precede a change in either Ireland's social structure or its electoral system. In the absence of such change, Irish politics may continue to be characterized by instability in the voting habits of the electorate and, ironically, by an image of stagnation.

NOTES

1. In this paper 'Ireland' will sometimes be used instead of 'the Republic of Ireland'. Use of the abbreviation is prompted solely by considerations of style and is without political connotations.

2. The June 1927 election results have been taken from the Irish Independent of 11-15 June 1927. For the September 1927 results the Oireachtas Companion and Saorstát Guide for 1930 was used; the 1939 Parliamentary Handbook provided the results of the elections of 1932, 1933, 1937 and 1938, and the 1943 and 1944 results were taken from the 1945 Parliamentary Handbook. Official returns, published by the Stationery Office, Dublin, are available for elections since 1948.

One modification has been made to the returns as published: votes cast for James Dillon in Monaghan at the elections of 1943 to 1951 inclusive have been taken as Fine Gael votes even though he was nominally an Independent. He had been Fine Gael's deputy leader until in 1942 he left the party after failing to win support for his proposal that Ireland enter the war. Only in 1943 did Fine Gael put up a candidate — who won 2.8 percent of the votes — against him. He rejoined the party in 1952 and led it from 1959 to 1965, clear evidence of how close in spirit he remained to Fine Gael while nominally outside the party. In line with accepted practice, votes cast for candidates described as 'Farmers' at the 1943 election have been taken as Clann na Talmhan votes, and National Labour votes in 1944 and 1948 have been added to the official Labour votes.

3. For full details of the sources of the ecological variables see Gallagher (1974 : 175-76).

4. The derivation of the equations was outlined in section I. The coefficients presented are the semi-standardized coefficients, and relate standard deviation units of the ecological variables to percentage units of the dependent variable. Thus, for example in June 1927 an increase in the proportion of Irish speakers of one standard

deviation of *that* variable corresponded to an increase of 2.56 percent in Fianna Fáil's strength.

5. The full correlation matrix is presented in Gallagher (1974 : 24-26).

6. The 'most agricultural areas' used here correspond closely, though not exactly, to the operational definition of the 'periphery' employed by Garvin (1974).

7. Sinn Féin won 3.63 percent of the votes in the June election but did not stand in September.

8. Fianna Fáil regarded the Senate, which especially in its early years contained a large number of ex-Unionists, as being composed of 'a certain class that could not get that power if they had to go before the people at a free election and get the people to vote them into office' (the words of Lemasss, quoted in O'Sullivan, 1940 : 232; cf. ibid. 233-34, 270).

9. This change, remarkable though little remarked upon, emphasizes the danger, when analysing Irish election results, of studying only the national result. The phenomenon of uniform swing, a feature of British electoral behaviour at least until recently (Butler and Stokes, 1969 : 135), is absent from Irish elections.

10. Labour had attempted to disarm such charges only five years earlier; in 1939 it modified some of the socialist rhetoric in its 1936 constitution after pressure from the Hierarchy acting through the Irish National Teachers' Organization (see Whyte, 1971 : 82-84).

11. An exception is perhaps Sinn Féin, which stood at four of the elections during the period, including the first and the most recent. As a political party, however, its existence would be better described as sporadic than continuous.

12. The division was on a vote of no confidence in the government – had it succeeded, a Labour-National League coalition would have been formed. In the event the National League member, John Jinks, did not vote, the motion was tied, and on the Speaker's casting vote Cumann na nGaedheal remained in office. Jinks earned fame and derision for his absence from the Dáil when the vote was taken, for which a number of explanations, some highly colourful, have been offered. It should be noted that Captain Redmond's father, John Redmond, was foremost among those urging Irishmen to join the British army during the First World War.

13. Redmond, who sat for Waterford, was the Irish Parliamentary Party's only successful candidate in the twenty-six county area at the 1918 election, and was elected as an Independent in 1923 and as a Cumann na nGaedheal deputy in 1932. Coburn (Louth) was returned as an Independent in 1932 and 1933 and for Fine Gael from 1937 to 1954. On the other hand a purely party vote for the National League did exist – its Donegal candidate, an ex-Irish Parliamentary Party M.P. at Westminster, won nearly 6,000 votes for the National League in June 1927 but had collected only 900 in 1923 when he stood as an Independent.

14. In fact correlation of the two parties' support at the election produces a negative coefficient ($r = -0.22$), showing that Sinn Féin tended to be weak where Fianna Fáil was strong.

15. The correlations for Cumann na nGaedheal and Farmers are significant at the 0.05 level. It must be borne in mind that some Centre Party candidates had stood in 1932 as Farmers or Independents, so it can be expected that they brought much of their support across with them.

16. Whereas in 1948 it stood in 16 constituencies, in 1951 it stood in only four (in Galway, Mayo and Roscommon). It polled very strongly in these constituencies, winning an average of about 31 percent of the votes in each and about 3 percent of the total votes cast in the country, but since it had no strength in each of the other

36 constituencies its vote was so far from being normally distributed that any correlation-based analysis of its support would be pointless.

17. Certainly most of its leaders fell into one category or the other. The party leader, Seán MacBride, was by 1948 'half in, half out' of the IRA, of which he was a former Chief of Staff, and the Clann sparked the enthusiasm of some of the more 'political' IRA members. It also attracted a number of prominent socialists like Noel Browne and Jack McQuillan. See Bell (1972 : 288-89), Coogan (1970 : 259-60) and Manning (1972 : 101).

18. See Chubb (1963) and (1974 : 213-15), Whyte (1966 : especially 6-23), and Keane (1967) for a fictional treatment of the subject. On 'broker politics' generally see Bax (1970), Garvin (1974), Gibbon and Higgins (1974) and Schmitt (1973).

19. Sacks's is the only Irish electoral study to use units smaller than the constituency. He was able to examine records made by party organizers at each pooling booth — when the counting is carried out the voting slips are 'fleetingly expos(ed) to the local politicians'.

20. These counties are Cavan, Donegal, Monaghan and Wicklow, with respectively 11.7, 13.7, 14.2 and 12.5 percent non-Catholics in 1961. The next most Protestant county was Dublin, where 7.6 percent of the population were non-Catholics. In Ireland the terms 'Protestant' and 'non-Catholic' amount to practically the same thing numerically: in 1961 fewer than 15,000 of the population of almost three million were neither Catholic nor Protestant.

21. The upsurge of support for Independents in 1973 does not indicate a change in Protestants' voting habits. Over two-thirds of the votes won by Independents in the four most Protestant counties were won by two strongly 'republican' candidates, Neil Blaney in Donegal North-East and Paudge Brennan in Wicklow, both of whom had been expelled from Fianna Fáil in 1970.

22. The figures do not cancel out because of minor changes in the strengths of Sinn Féin, Clann na Poblachta and Clann na Talmhan between the two elections.

23. These areas are Cavan, Clare, Cork City, Cork County, Donegal, Dublin City, Dublin County, Galway, Kerry, Laoghis-Offaly, Limerick, Louth, Mayo, Monaghan, Roscommon, Sligo-Leitrim, Tipperary, Waterford, Wexford, Wicklow, Carlow-Kildare-Kilkenny and Long-Meath-Westmeath.

24. The average number of voters in these areas over the fourteen elections varies considerably, from 26,000 in Wicklow to 162,000 in Dublin City, and consequently each case has been weighted by its average number of voters on the ground that a change in a party's strength in Dublin City is more significant than a similar change in its strength in Wicklow. In fact this weighting makes very little difference to the values of the correlation coefficients.

25. Pomper (1967 : 538). If the change proves permanent the election is 'realigning'; if temporary it is 'deviant'.

REFERENCES

AYEARST, M. (1971) The Republic of Ireland. London: University of London Press.

BAX, M. (1970) 'Patronage Irish Style: Irish politicians as brokers', Sociologische Gids, Vol. 17 (3): 179-91.

BELL, J.B. (1972) The Secret Army. London: Sphere.

BUSTEED, M.A. and H. MASON (1970) 'Irish Labour in the 1969 Election', Political Studies, Vol. 18 (3): 373-79.

BUTLER, D. and D. STOKES (1969) Political Change in Britain. London: Macmillan.

CHUBB, B. (1957) 'The Independent Member in Ireland', Political Studies, Vol. 5 (2): 131-39.

CHUBB, B. (1959) 'Ireland 1957', in D. E. Butler (ed.) Elections Abroad. London: Macmillan.

CHUBB, B. (1963)' "Going about persecuting Civil Servants": The Role of the Irish Parliamentary Representative', Political Studies, Vol. 11 (3): 272-86.

CHUBB, B. (ed) (1964) A Source Book of Irish Government. Dublin: Institute of Public Administration.

CHUBB, B. (1974) The Government and Politics of Ireland. London: Oxford University Press.

CLARKSON, J.D. (1926) Labour and Nationalism in Ireland. New York: Columbia University Press.

COOGAN, T.P. (1966) Ireland Since the Rising. London: Pall Mall Press.

COOGAN, T.P. (1970) The IRA. London: Pall Mall Press.

EDWARDS, O.D. (ed) (1969) Conor Cruise O'Brien Introduces Ireland. London: Andre Deutsch.

FARRELL, B. (1970) 'Labour and the Irish Political Party System: A Suggested Approach to Analysis', Economic and Social Review, Vol. 1 (4): 477-502.

FARRELL, B. (1971a) Chairman or Chief? Dublin: Gill and Macmillan.

FARRELL, B. (1971b) 'Dáil Deputies: "The 1969 Generation" ', Economic and Social Review, Vol. 2 (3): 309-27.

FIANNA FAIL (1960) The Story of Fianna Fáil: First Phase. Dublin: Fianna Fáil.

FINE GAEL (1965) Fine Gael Policy 1965: 'Towards a Just Society'. Dublin: Fine Gael.

GALLAGHER, M. (1974) 'The Bases of Support for Political Parties in the Republic of Ireland 1927-1973'. University of Strathclyde: M.Sc. dissertation.

GALLAGHER, M. (1975) 'Disproportionality in a Proportional Representation System: The Irish Experience', Political Studies, Vol. 23 (4): 501-13.

GALTUNG, J. (1967) Theory and Methods of Social Research. London: George Allen and Unwin.

GARVIN, T. (1974) 'Political Cleavages, Party Politics and Urbanisation in Ireland: The case of the periphery-dominated centre', European Journal of Political Research, Vol. 2 (4): 307-27.

GIBBON, P. and M.D. HIGGINS (1974) 'Patronage, Tradition and Modernisation: The Case of the Irish "Gombeenman" ', Economic and Social Review, Vol. 6 (1): 27-44.

GWYNN, D. (1928) The Irish Free State 1922-1927. London: Macmillan.

HART, I. (1970) 'Public Opinion on Civil Servants and the Role and Power of the Individual in the Local Community', Administration, Vol. 18 (4): 375-91.

INGLIS, B. (1965) The Story of Ireland (2nd edn). London: Faber and Faber.

KEANE, J. (1967) Letters of a Successful T.D. Cork: Mercier Press.

LYNCH, P. (1969) 'The Economic Scene' in Edwards (1969) pp. 71-82.

LYONS, F.S.L. (1971) Ireland Since the Famine. London: Weidenfeld and Nicolson.

LYSAGHT, D.R.O'C. (1970) The Republic of Ireland. Cork: Mercier Press.

MACKIE, T.T. (1971) Some Aspects of Electoral Change in Italy 1948-1968. University of Strathclyde: M.Sc. dissertation.

MANNING, M. (1970) The Blueshirts. Dublin: Gill and Macmillan.

MANNING, M. (1972) Irish Political Parties. Dublin: Gill and Macmillan.

MANSERGH, N. (1934) The Irish Free State. London: George Allen and Unwin.

McCRACKEN, J.L. (1958) Representative Government in Ireland. London: Oxford University Press.

MEENAN, J. (1969) 'The Irish Economy During the War', in Nowlan and Williams (1969) pp. 28-38.

MITCHELL, A. (1974) Labour in Irish Politics. Dublin: Irish University Press.

MOSS, W. (1933) Political Parties in the Irish Free State. New York: Columbia University Press.

MUNGER, F. (1975) 'The Legitimacy of Opposition: The Change of Government in Ireland in 1932', SAGE Professional Paper in Contemporary Political Sociology, Vol. 1, 06-006. London and Beverly Hills: SAGE Publications.

MURPHY, J.A. (1969) 'The Irish Party System, 1938-51', in Nowlan and Williams (1969) pp. 147-66.

MURPHY, J.A. (1975) Ireland in the Twentieth Century. Dublin: Gill and Macmillan.

NEVIN, D. (1969) 'Industry and Labour', in Nowlan and Williams (1969) pp. 94-108.

NOWLAN, K.B. and T.D. WILLIAMS (eds) (1969) Ireland in the War Years and After, 1939-51. Dublin: Gill and Macmillan.

O'LEARY, C. (1961) The Irish Republic. Notre Dame: University of Notre Dame Press.

O'SULLIVAN, D. (1940) The Irish Free State and its Senate. London: Faber and Faber.

POMPER, G. (1967) 'Classification of Presidential Elections', Journal of Politics, Vol. 29 (3): 535-66.

PYNE, P.P. (1969-70) 'The Third Sinn Féin Party: 1923-1926', in two parts: Economic and Social Review, Vol. 1 (1): 29-50 and 1 (2): 229-57.

ROBINSON, W.S. (1950) 'Ecological Correlations and the Behaviour of Individuals', American Sociological Review, Vol. 15: 351-57.

ROSE, R. (ed.) (1974) Electoral Behaviour; A Comparative Handbook. New York: Free Press.

RUMPF, E. (1959) Nationalismus und Sozialismus in Irland. Meisenheim am Glan: Anton Hain.

SACKS, P.M. (1970) 'Bailiwicks, Locality and Religion: Three Elements in an Irish Dáil Constituency Election', Economic and Social Review, Vol. 1 (4): 531-54.

SCHMITT, D.E. (1973) The Irony of Irish Democracy. Lexington: D.C. Heath.

VINEY, M. and O.D. EDWARDS (1969) 'Parties and Power' in Edwards (1969) pp. 83-103.

WHYTE, J. (1966) 'Dáil Deputies: Their Work, Its Difficulties, Possible Remedies'. Dublin: Tuairim Pamphlet No. 15.

WHYTE, J.H. (1971) Church and State in Modern Ireland. Dublin: Gill and Macmillan.

WHYTE. J.H. (1974) 'Ireland: Politics Without Social Bases' in Rose (1974) pp. 619-51.

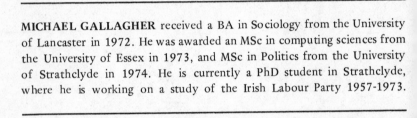

MICHAEL GALLAGHER received a BA in Sociology from the University of Lancaster in 1972. He was awarded an MSc in computing sciences from the University of Essex in 1973, and MSc in Politics from the University of Strathclyde in 1974. He is currently a PhD student in Strathclyde, where he is working on a study of the Irish Labour Party 1957-1973.